1 Workbook

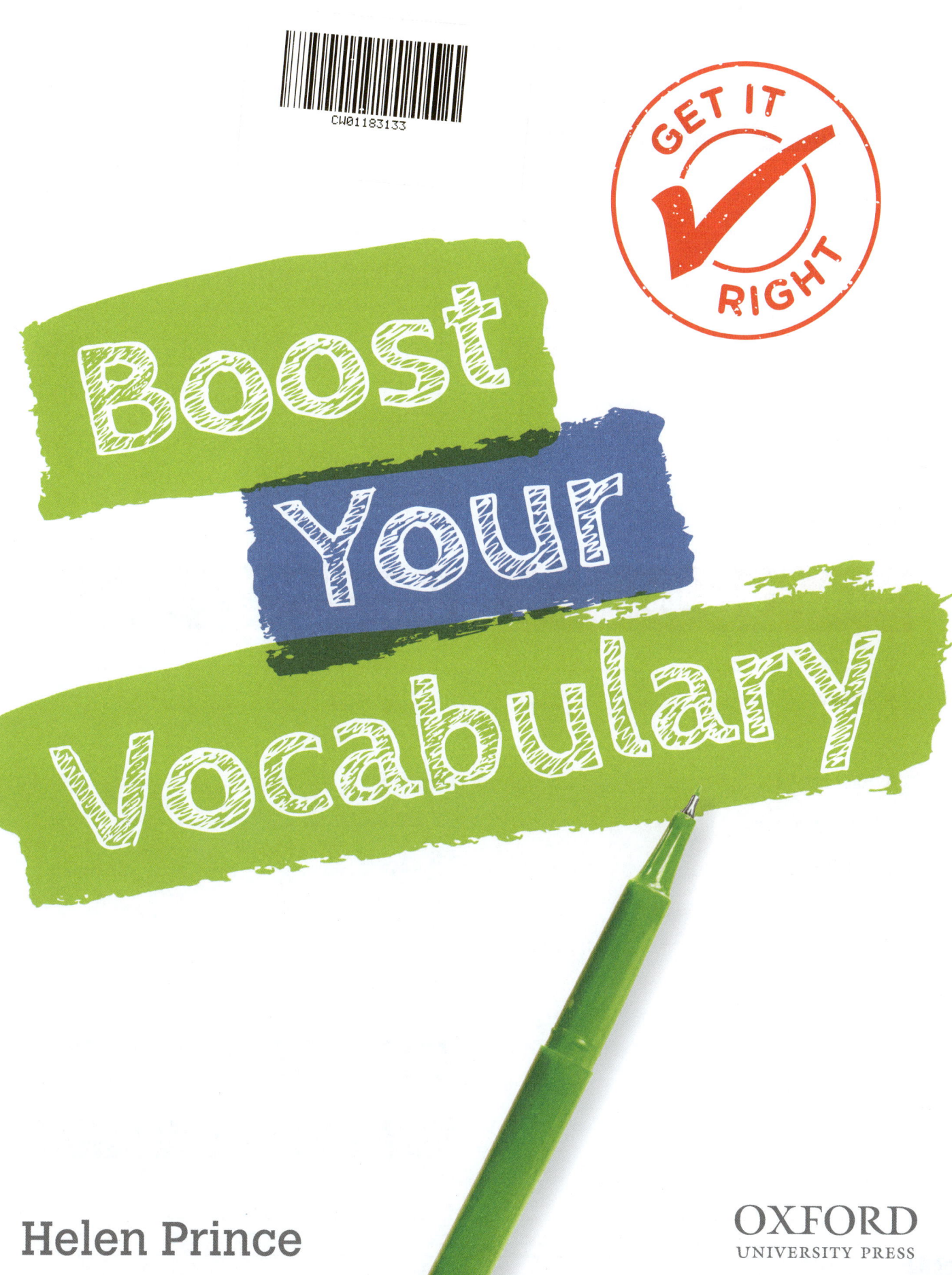

Boost Your Vocabulary

Helen Prince

OXFORD UNIVERSITY PRESS

GET IT RIGHT

Contents

Chapter 1: Conflict and control — 4

1. Fury 4
2. Sacrifice 6
3. Peril 8
4. Malice 10
5. Adversary 12
6. Ruthless 14
7. Persistent 16
8. Conceal 18
9. Deceit 20

Chapter 2: Mood and tone — 22

1. Solemn 22
2. Hostile 24
3. Melancholy 26
4. Bleak 28
5. Apprehensive 30
6. Sinister 32
7. Incredulous 34
8. Elated 36
9. Foreboding 38

Chapter 3: Individual and society — 40

1. Moral 40
2. Virtuous 42
3. Sentiment 44
4. Civilised 46
5. Prejudice 48
6. Benevolent 50
7. Betray 52
8. Industrious 54
9. Inferior 56

Chapter 4: Analysis and explanation — 58

1. Observe 58
2. Contrast 60
3. Characterise 62
4. Portray 64
5. Evaluate 66
6. Context 68
7. Conventional 70
8. Imply 72
9. Ambiguous 74

Word list — 76

Key terms glossary — 79

For answers go to www.oxfordsecondary.com/getitright-vocab/answers

Introduction

How this workbook will help you

The *Get It Right: Boost Your Vocabulary* series will introduce you to a range of exciting new words that will help to build your vocabulary. Each workbook features 36 ambitious words that will help you to read more difficult texts and to make your own writing more inspiring and powerful.

How this workbook is structured

The workbook contains 36 focus words, split across four chapters.

Each unit within a chapter will focus on a single word as a starting point. In each unit, you will find everything you need to help you understand the focus word and to enable you to use it confidently in your own writing. Each unit includes a simple definition and example sentences to help you understand the meaning, as well as interesting facts about where the word comes from and opportunities to explore other words with similar and opposite meanings.

The **Word list** at the end of the workbook provides definitions of all the synonyms (words with similar meanings) and antonyms (words with opposite meanings) covered throughout each unit.

Which features are included?

The workbook includes a range of activities to test your understanding of each focus word, with space to write your answers throughout.

- **Understanding the meaning** activities test your basic comprehension of the focus word.
- **Exploring the meaning** activities help you to explore the word in a deeper way by examining words with similar or opposite meanings (as part of a word web). You might also be asked to think about any feelings or ideas suggested by the word (connotations).
- **Reading skills** activities include a short text extract to show the word in context, alongside questions that help you to consider the effect of the writer's choices.
- **Writing skills** activities challenge you to use the focus word in your own writing across a range of non-fiction and creative writing tasks.

Each unit also includes a **Have your say** activity. These tasks can be completed individually or used as debate tasks and group discussions.

Throughout this workbook, **Tips** offer support and guidance for completing activities, while the **Word knowledge** feature provides interesting facts about the origins of the focus word.

Key literary and linguistic terms are emboldened throughout each unit. Definitions for these words are provided in the **Key terms glossary** at the end of the workbook.

3

Chapter 1: Conflict and control

 Fury

The **noun** 'fury' has two meanings:

1) a wild anger or rage
2) an extreme or uncontrollable force in nature.

In her *fury* she yelled at her friends. (noun)

They were terrified by the *fury* of the storm. (noun)

Other words in the same **word family** are:

- furious (**adjective**)
- furiously (**adverb**).

I was *furious* that someone had stolen my money. (adjective)

She pulled down the posters *furiously*. (adverb)

Word knowledge

In Greek mythology, there were three goddesses of revenge called the Furies. They punished people who committed crimes, focusing on children who disrespected their parents, liars, murderers, and people who sinned against the gods.

How does this information add to your understanding of the word 'fury'?

💬 Have your say

1) 'Fury is just lack of control.' How far do you agree with this statement?
2) Describe a furious moment from a book, TV or film. What triggered the fury?

Try to justify your ideas with examples to support your points.

✏️ Activity 1 — Understanding the meaning

1) Read the sentences below and tick those where forms of the word 'fury' are used correctly.

At 6 p.m., the shopkeeper shut the door to several furious customers.	
Her face relaxed with fury at the sight of the enormous birthday cake.	
The ship and its crew had to survive the full fury of a storm-force gale.	
The toddler threw a furious tantrum in the middle of the supermarket.	

2) Rewrite an incorrect sentence, replacing the form of the word 'fury' with a more suitable alternative.

....

....

4

Fury 1

✏ Activity 2 — Exploring the meaning

Look at the word web of **synonyms** for the noun 'fury'. Use the word list on pages 76–78 to look up any unfamiliar words.

1) Circle three synonyms that you think best describe a person's wild anger.

2) Tick three synonyms that you think best describe an extreme force in nature, such as violent weather.

3) Write a sentence using the noun 'fury' or one of its synonyms to describe someone's wild anger.

   ----

4) Write a sentence using the noun 'fury' or one of its synonyms to describe extreme weather.

Word web: fury — rage, wrath, savagery, turbulence, madness, ferocity

✏ Activity 3 — 'Fury' in context: reading skills

Read the extract below from *Smith* by Leon Garfield. Smith is a 12-year-old pickpocket living on the streets. One morning he spies a likely victim.

> At about half past ten of a cold December morning an old gentleman got furiously out of his **carriage**, in which he'd been trapped for an hour, shook his red fist at his helpless coachman and the roaring but motionless world, and began to stump up Ludgate Hill.
>
> '*Pick*-pocket! *Pick*-pocket!' shrieked the cathedral birds in a fury.
>
> **carriage** – a passenger vehicle pulled by horses

1) Why is the old gentleman so angry? Use evidence from the text to explain your answer.

   ----

2) If you were an actor, how might you demonstrate the word 'furiously' as you get out of your carriage? Think about facial **expression, gestures, posture,** words and noises.

   ----

3) How do the words 'furiously' and 'fury' build tension in this extract? What other words add to this feeling?

5

Chapter 1: Conflict and control

 Sacrifice

The **verb** 'sacrifice' has two meanings:

1) to give something up for something else you feel is more important
2) to kill something for a god.

> 'Friday night is my only free time and I won't *sacrifice* it for anything.' (verb)

> The Romans used to *sacrifice* cattle and sheep to their gods. (verb)

Other words in the same **word family** are:

- sacrifice (**noun**)
- sacrificial (**adjective**)
- sacrificially (**adverb**).

> We must all make *sacrifices* if we want to save enough money for our trip to Thailand next year. (noun)

> Giving up your seat to an elderly person on a busy bus is a *sacrificial* act. (adjective)

> The soldier served her country *sacrificially*. (adverb)

Word knowledge

The word 'sacrifice' comes from the Latin word *sacer*, meaning 'holy'.

What other religious words come from the same origin as 'sacrifice'? Use a dictionary to help you.

 Have your say

Is making a sacrifice a good or bad thing? Give reasons for your answer.

Activity 1 — Understanding the meaning

1) Complete the sentences below by adding the correct form of the word 'sacrifice'.

   a) The enormous _____ was appreciated by the whole team.

   b) She _____ her break to help her teacher clear up the mess.

   c) They made a _____ offering to please their god.

   d) Carers work _____ for the good of others.

2) Write your own sentence using the word 'sacrifice'. You can use it as a noun or a verb.

   _____

   _____

6

Sacrifice 2

✏ Activity 2 Exploring the meaning

Look at the word web of **synonyms** for the verb 'sacrifice'. Use the word list on pages 76–78 to look up any unfamiliar words.

1) Choose two of the synonyms for 'sacrifice'. Write a short definition for each word in the table below. Use a dictionary to check your definition.

Word	Definition

2) Choose four of the words in the word web. Do they have positive or negative **connotations**? Add the words to the table below, along with your reasoning. If you think the word has both positive and negative connotations, you can add it to both columns.

Positive connotations	Negative connotations
	forfeit – this word suggests that something has been taken away as a punishment

✏ Activity 3 'Sacrifice' in context: writing skills

Imagine your class is going to spend a week at an outdoor adventure centre. The staff have asked all students to leave their phones at home. Do you think the sacrifice is worth it to go on the trip?

On separate paper, write 100 words to persuade your class of your view. Use the word 'sacrifice' and some of the synonyms above in your writing.

Tip

Try to:
- use **emotive language**
- include **rhetorical questions**.

7

Chapter 1: Conflict and control

3 Peril

The **noun** 'peril' means a serious risk or great danger.

> The fisherman knew all about the *perils* of the sea. (noun)

Other words in the same **word family** are:

- perilous (**adjective**)
- perilously (**adverb**).

> They began their *perilous* journey home along the icy mountain path. (adjective)

> The horse stood *perilously* close to the edge of the cliff. (adverb)

They began their **perilous** journey home along the icy mountain path.

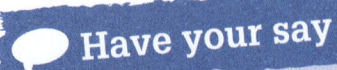 **Have your say**

Discuss what a perilous situation might be for:

- a bus driver
- a toddler
- a hospital
- a cruise ship.

✏️ Activity 1   Understanding the meaning

1) Complete the sentences below by adding the correct form of the word 'peril'.

   a) Lin had never known such a _____ time; everything in her life seemed so uncertain.

   b) The weather created a sense of _____, with the heavy rain crashing onto the roof.

   c) The marathon runner felt _____ close to giving up, but the thought of victory kept her going.

   d) Despite the _____ they faced, the explorers were determined to get to the summit.

2) Write your own sentence using the word 'peril'.

   _____

   _____

8

Peril 3

✏ Activity 2   Exploring the meaning

Look at the word web of **synonyms** for the noun 'peril'. Use the word list on pages 76–78 to look up any unfamiliar words.

1) Rank the level of 'peril' in each synonym, numbering them 1 to 6 on the word web (1 being the least 'perilous').

2) Write two sentences. One should include your least 'perilous' word. The other should include your most 'perilous' word. Try to show the different levels of 'peril' in your sentences.

Word web: peril (centre), with synonyms: danger, risk, hazard, uncertainty, pitfall, jeopardy.

✏ Activity 3   'Peril' in context: reading skills

Read the extract below from *Hints to Lady Travellers* by Lillias Campbell Davidson. In this extract, a Victorian explorer advises her readers to prepare for problems during their travels, but also warns them against becoming over-anxious.

> Never anticipate accidents, though you prepare against them. I mean, don't feel convinced, every journey that you set out upon, that peril lurks in **ambush** in your path. Don't see collision in every jolt of the train, and scent shipwreck in each lurch of the **steamer**. Travelling under such circumstances will become neither an enjoyment nor a benefit, and you had better remain at home all your days with a fire-escape tied to your window and a burglar-alarm ready to your hand.
>
> **ambush** – surprise attack
> **steamer** – boat powered by steam

1) What two examples of peril or disaster are described?

----

2) How would you describe the author's **tone**? Circle one of the words below or write your own.

    serious   scary   humorous   sorrowful   ------------------------

3) How does the author use **personification** to bring the word 'peril' to life?

Chapter 1: Conflict and control

 Malice

The **noun** 'malice' means the wish to hurt or upset someone.

> Their actions were foolish but there was no *malice* intended. (noun)

Other words in the same **word family** are:
- malicious (**adjective**)
- maliciously (**adverb**).

> The festival had to close early due to *malicious* damage to the displays. (adjective)

> It was a *maliciously* hurtful thing to say. (adverb)

Word knowledge

The word 'malice' comes from the Latin word *malus*, meaning 'evil' or 'wicked'.

Writers often name characters to give the reader a clue to their personality. What does the name 'Malfoy' suggest about a character?

💬 Have your say

It has been said that 'if malice had a shape, it would be a boomerang'.
Do you agree or disagree with this idea? Why?

Tip

What does a boomerang do that might also happen to those who show malice?

✏️ Activity 1 Understanding the meaning

1) Read the sentences below and tick those where forms of the word 'malice' are used correctly.

Their malicious gossip created a happy and friendly atmosphere.	
The band felt no malice towards their manager when she left.	
The kind and malicious children asked the new pupil to join in with their game.	
The tiger stared at its prey with quiet malice.	

2) Rewrite an incorrect sentence, replacing the form of the word 'malice' with a more suitable alternative.

10

Malice

✏️ Activity 2 Exploring the meaning

The **prefix** 'mal-' can be added to many words to mean 'bad' or 'badly'. Look at the words on the tree branches that start with the prefix 'mal-'. Use the word list on pages 76–78 to look up any unfamiliar words.

1) Read the definitions below and decide which links best with each word.

a) badly made or developed

b) poor health due to not eating healthy food or enough food

c) smelly

d) wrong advice or treatment given by a professional person

e) to treat a person with cruelty

f) a failure to work properly

Tree branch words: malodorous, malnutrition, malfunction, malpractice, maltreat, malformed

2) Choose one of the words. Write a sentence including that word. Try to show the exact meaning of the word in your sentence.

_____

_____

_____

✏️ Activity 3 'Malice' in context: writing skills

Imagine a malicious character in a story. On separate paper, complete the paragraph below, describing at least one situation that revealed their malice.

She was quiet and secretive, but I soon discovered the terrible malice that riddled her personality. I first noticed it when …

Tip

Describe the emotions that the character's malice makes you feel, such as uneasy, shocked or apprehensive.

11

Chapter 1: Conflict and control

5 Adversary

The **noun** 'adversary' means an enemy or someone you are competing against.

> She crossed the finish line just half a second behind her *adversary*. (noun)

Another word in the same **word family** is the **adjective** 'adversarial'.

> The lawyers enjoyed being *adversarial* in the courtroom. (adjective)

Word knowledge

'Adversary' comes from the Latin word *adversus*, meaning 'turned against', 'opposite' or 'hostile'.

How does this information add to your understanding of the word 'adversary'?

💬 Have your say

There are lots of examples of adversaries in TV, sports, films and books; for example, Batman and the Joker are adversaries. Name four more pairs or groups of adversaries that you can think of.

✏️ Activity 1 — Understanding the meaning

1) Using the information above, complete the following grid with more information about the word 'adversary'. Some ideas have been added to help you.

Definition What does the word adversary mean?	**Characteristics** How might an adversary behave? • Being competitive
Examples Where might someone meet an adversary? • A sports competition	**Non-example** Who isn't an adversary? • Someone who helps you succeed

Adversary

Adversary 5

Activity 2 — Exploring the meaning

Look at the word web of **synonyms** for the noun 'adversary'. Use the word list on pages 76–78 to look up any unfamiliar words.

Word web synonyms: combatant, rival, enemy, adversary, foe, antagonist, opponent

1) Circle the synonym that sounds most dangerous. Explain your answer.

   ----

2) Tick the synonym that sounds least dangerous. Explain your answer.

   ----

3) Choose one of the other synonyms. Write a sentence including that synonym. Try to show the exact meaning of the word in your sentence.

Activity 3 — 'Adversary' in context: reading skills

Read the extract below from *Noble Conflict* by Malorie Blackman. Kaspar, who has been trained as a fighter in the Academy, is suddenly facing his first real enemy: a deadly ninja.

> Kaspar dropped into a combat **stance**, ready to go hand-to-hand. The sweetish taste of adrenalin filled his mouth. This was it – kill or be killed. His first real experience of up-close-and-personal combat outside of the Academy. Kaspar forced himself to slow his breathing, never for a moment taking his eyes off his adversary. Their eyes locked.
>
> **stance** – position

1) Who is Kaspar's adversary in this extract?

   ----

2) What does 'their eyes locked' mean?

   ----

3) How does the phrase 'their eyes locked' add to the adversarial atmosphere?

Chapter 1: Conflict and control

 Ruthless

The **adjective** 'ruthless' means determined to get what you want and not caring if you hurt other people.

> The gardener was *ruthless* with the weeds; they were attacked and on the compost heap in moments. (adjective)

Other words in the same **word family** are:

- ruthlessness (**noun**)
- ruthlessly (**adverb**).

> Her *ruthlessness* and ambition to win at all costs led to her taking the trophy. (noun)

> The fire *ruthlessly* attacked the forest, leaving nothing but blackened, charred earth. (adverb)

Word knowledge

'Ruthless' comes from the Middle English word *ruthe*, meaning 'pity'. It also contains the **suffix** '-less', meaning 'without', so the whole word means 'without pity'.

How does this information add to your understanding of the word 'ruthless'?

💬 Have your say

'Everyone needs to be ruthless sometimes.'

Do you agree with this statement? Why/Why not?

✏️ Activity 1 — Understanding the meaning

The word 'ruthless' can describe a person who is focused, determined and not distracted by anything. This means that sometimes ruthlessness can be seen as a positive quality.

1) Read the sentences below and tick whether the word 'ruthless' is used as a positive or negative quality.

Sentences	Positive quality	Negative quality
She was so ruthless that her friends stopped speaking to her.		
His ruthless attitude helped him to win an Olympic gold medal.		
They were ruthless in uncovering all the lies in the group.		
It took years for the nation to recover from the ruthless actions of the dictator.		

2) Write two more sentences, one using 'ruthless' as a positive quality and one using it as a negative quality.

14

Rutshless

Activity 2 — Exploring the meaning

The suffix '-less' can be added to many words to mean 'without'. Look at the words on the tree branches that end with the suffix '-less'. Use the word list on pages 76–78 to look up any unfamiliar words.

Tree words: cheerless, tactless, remorseless, fruitless, doubtless, heartless

1) Read the definitions below and decide which links best with each word.

a) without joy or happiness

b) without a good outcome

c) showing no guilt

d) certainty

e) not feeling any pity or sympathy

f) insensitive

2) Choose one of the words. Write a sentence including that word. Try to show the exact meaning of the word in your sentence.

Activity 3 — 'Ruthless' in context: writing skills

An American sports commentator and former professional football player gave this advice:

> "You tell everyone or anyone that has ever doubted, thought they did not measure up or wanted to quit, you tell them to *look up, get up and don't ever give up*."

Think about how this quotation links to the positive ideas for 'ruthlessness'. On separate paper and using these ideas, write a short speech to motivate your favourite team or sportsperson and make them believe they are the best!

15

Chapter 1: Conflict and control

7 Persistent

The **adjective** 'persistent' has two meanings:
1) determined to continue doing something and refusing to give up
2) continuing or constant.

> He was *persistent* in his training; he ran every day. (adjective)

> *Persistent* wildfires have damaged many areas of woodland. (adjective)

Other words in the same **word family** are:
- persist (**verb**)
- persistence (**noun**)
- persistently (**adverb**).

> If your fever *persists* for more than a few days, see your doctor. (verb)

> Their *persistence* and hard work was rewarded with a party. (noun)

> Why are you *persistently* late to work? (adverb)

He was **persistent** in his training; he ran every day.

Have your say

'A river cuts through rock not because of its power but because of its persistence.'

What can we learn about persistence from this idea?

Word knowledge

'Persistent' comes from the Latin word *per* meaning 'through' and *sistere* meaning 'to stand'.

How does this information add to your understanding of the word 'persistent'?

✏ Activity 1 — Understanding the meaning

Using the information above, complete the following grid with more information about the word 'persistent'. Some ideas have been added to help you.

Definition What does the word persistent mean?	**Characteristics** How might a persistent person behave? • Never giving up even if you fail
Examples When might someone be persistent?	**Non-example** What isn't persistent behaviour? • Giving up straight away

Persistent

16

Persistent 7

✏ Activity 2 Exploring the meaning

Look at the word web of **synonyms** for the adjective 'persistent'. Use the word list on pages 76–78 to look up any unfamiliar words.

Word web synonyms for **persistent**: steadfast, incessant, enduring, relentless, endless, tenacious.

1) Decide which of the synonyms have positive **connotations** and which have negative connotations.

Positive connotations	Negative connotations

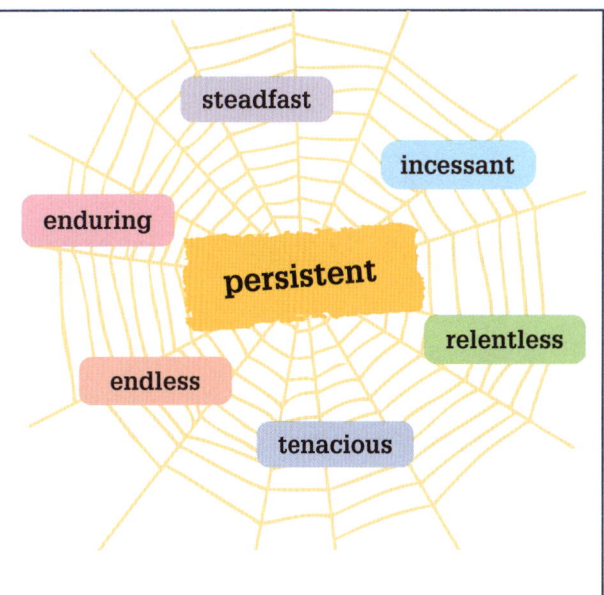

2) Write two sentences, using a positive synonym in one sentence and a negative synonym in the other.

_____

_____

_____

_____

✏ Activity 3 'Persistent' in context: reading skills

The extract below is from an article about persistence.

> Persistence is a quality that many successful people have demonstrated.
>
> Have you heard that anything worth having is worth working for? It's true. There are lots of examples of heroes of ours who persisted and stayed on course, despite failure:
> - It took Thomas Edison 1000 attempts before inventing the light bulb. His teachers also told him growing up that he was too stupid to learn anything.
> - Michael Jordan was cut from his high school basketball team for not being good enough.

1) What does it mean to 'stay on course'?

_____

2) How do the personal stories above add to your understanding of persistence?

_____

3) How can persistence help you to achieve your goals?

_____

_____

17

Chapter 1: Conflict and control

 Conceal

The **verb** 'conceal' has two meanings:

1) to hide something   2) to keep something secret.

> The actor tried to *conceal* his disappointment when the winner was announced. (verb)

> *Concealing* their stash of chocolate, the children ran upstairs giggling. (verb)

Other words in the same **word family** are:

- concealment (**noun**)
- concealed (**adjective**).

> The police decided that the *concealment* of the truth had been done on purpose. (noun)

> Finally they found the *concealed* door. (adjective)

Word knowledge

'Conceal' comes from the Latin words *con*, meaning 'completely', and *celare* meaning 'to hide' or 'keep secret'.

How does this information add to your understanding of the word 'conceal'?

💬 Have your say

Imagine you discover your friend has concealed something from you. Think about:

- how you might feel about your friend's actions
- what might happen once you discover the whole story.

✏️ Activity 1 | Understanding the meaning

1) Read the sentences below and tick those where forms of the word 'conceal' are used correctly.

As the driver was arrested, she concealed her bag under a blanket.
Opening the new science labs, the headteacher smiled at the students to conceal his happiness.
The tourists cheered and clapped as the cruise ship arrived to conceal their excitement.
The reporter had a notebook and microphone concealed in her back pocket.

2) Rewrite an incorrect sentence, replacing the form of the word 'conceal' with a more suitable alternative.

18

Conceal

Activity 2 Exploring the meaning

Look at the word web of **synonyms** for the verb 'conceal'. Use the word list on pages 76–78 to look up any unfamiliar words.

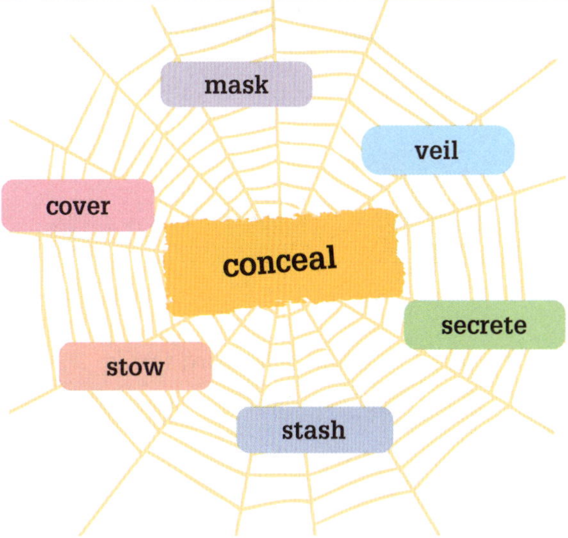

1) Decide which words are most likely to be used in each **context** and write them in the table. Note that some words may belong in more than one context.

To disguise	To commit crime	To keep a secret

Word web: conceal — mask, veil, cover, secrete, stow, stash

2) Choose one word from each context and write a sentence including that word. Think carefully about how to include the context in your sentences.

Activity 3 'Conceal' in context: reading skills

Read the extract below from 'Lady in Blue, Unidentified' by Terence Blacker. The story tells of a man investigating supernatural activity in an old house.

> After tea, I walked by the **moat**, turning over in my mind the details of the Reverend Radcliffe's account. So deep in thought was I that I soon found myself by the small **chantry chapel**, which was almost concealed by trees on the far side of the drive. It was from there, as the evening gloom closed in on me, that I heard the sound of a human voice, female, singing quietly.
>
> **moat** – body of water surrounding a castle or large house
> **chantry chapel** – part of a church dedicated to the memory of a person or family

1) What made it difficult to see the small chantry chapel?

----

2) How does this description of the evening add to the idea of concealment?

19

Chapter 1: Conflict and control

9 Deceit

The **noun** 'deceit' means the act of making a person believe something that is not true, or tricking them.

> Hidden beneath his smile lay a web of *deceit* and trickery. (noun)

Other words in the same **word family** are:
- deceitful (**adjective**)
- deceitfully (**adverb**)
- deceive (**verb**).

> The politician's *deceitful* behaviour was uncovered by the newspapers. (adjective)

> They were charged with taking money *deceitfully* from their employer. (adverb)

> Under the cover of darkness, it was easier to *deceive* the hunter and get away. (verb)

The politician's **deceitful** behaviour was uncovered by the newspapers.

Have your say

Imagine two students are caught trying to pass a test deceitfully.

1) Who do you think the students intend to deceive by cheating in a test?
2) Explain why being deceitful in a test won't help them succeed in the long term.

Activity 1 — Understanding the meaning

1) Complete the sentences below by adding the correct form of the word 'deceit'.

   a) His _____ led to his downfall.

   b) Several attempts to _____ the referee were uncovered.

   c) My neighbour's _____ behaviour had been going on for years.

   d) Harry _____ took his sister's chocolate bar from the cupboard.

2) Write two sentences using different forms of the word 'deceit'.

   _____

   _____

Deceit 9

✏️ Activity 2 — Exploring the meaning

Look at the word web for **synonyms** for the noun 'deceit'. Use the word list on pages 76–78 to look up any unfamiliar words.

1) Rank the synonyms from least serious to most serious, numbering them 1 to 6 on the word web (1 being the least serious).

2) Choose three words, including the most and least serious, and explain why you have ranked them as you have.

   ----

3) Write a sentence using your most serious word.

Word web: **deceit** — dishonesty, guile, pretence, trickery, fraud, cheating

✏️ Activity 3 — 'Deceit' in context: reading skills

In *Marmion: A Tale of Flodden Field*, Sir Walter Scott reflects on how telling lies is like spinning a spider's web.

> Oh what a tangled web we weave,
> When first we practise to deceive!

1) What do you think Scott is suggesting about deceit and lies by using the **metaphor** of a spider's web? Think about the purpose of a web, how sticky it is and how something can get caught up in it!

   ----

2) On separate paper, plan a short story that demonstrates Scott's ideas about lies and deceit. Think carefully about your main character, what deception they plan and how they get tangled/caught out in that deceit.

21

Chapter 2: Mood and tone

Solemn

The **adjective** 'solemn' has two meanings:
1) serious and not smiling
2) formal or dignified.

His *solemn* face matched his formal suit: grey and serious. (adjective)

The knights swore a *solemn* oath to protect the kingdom. (adjective)

Other words in the same **word family** are:
- solemnity (**noun**)
- solemnly (**adverb**).

The courtroom had an air of *solemnity*. (noun)

She walked *solemnly* towards the door, knowing she would never return. (adverb)

Word knowledge

'Solemn' comes from the Latin word *sollemnis*, meaning 'formal', 'traditional', or 'used in religious ceremonies'.

How does this information add to your understanding of the word 'solemn'?

Tip

Think about how your **tone** and word choices can add meaning and solemnity.

Have your say

In the most solemn way possible, describe the theft of your friend's bike from outside your house.

Activity 1 — Understanding the meaning

1) Complete the sentences below by adding the correct form of the word 'solemn'.

   a) In silent rows, the _____ teenagers filed into the assembly hall.

   b) An air of _____ fell on the team, as their national anthem began to play.

   c) With a serious and _____ tone, the lawyer began to read the statement.

   d) _____ , the actors moved to the front of the stage.

2) Write your own sentence using the word 'solemn'.

   _____

   _____

Solemn 1

✏ Activity 2 Exploring the meaning

Look at the word web for **synonyms** for the adjective 'solemn'. Use the word list on pages 76–78 to look up any unfamiliar words.

Word web synonyms for **solemn**: stern, sombre, reflective, dignified, formal, intense.

1) Describe the settings below, using the synonyms from the word web.

police station	The atmosphere was <u>intense</u>, just like the police officer's <u>sombre</u> face.
exam hall	
doctor's waiting room	
parents' evening	

2) Think of two **antonyms** for the word 'solemn'. Write them down and write your own definition for each of them.

✏ Activity 3 'Solemn' in context: writing skills

On separate paper, write a news article about a solemn public event that has taken place in a town or city near where you live. Follow the steps below.

1) Decide on the event. It might be:
   - a ceremony to give awards
   - a traditional religious or cultural event
   - a formal celebration of someone's life or a historic event.

2) Think of a heading for your article, then give details about when, where, and why the event took place, including who was there.

3) Explain what happened at the event. Describe the **mood** and **tone** of the occasion for your readers, including the word 'solemn' and some of the synonyms above.

23

Chapter 2: Mood and tone

2 Hostile

The **adjective** 'hostile' has three meanings:

1) unfriendly and angry
2) opposed to or against something
3) to do with an enemy.

> The *hostile* atmosphere made them feel very unwelcome. (adjective)

> They loved their old house so they were *hostile* to the idea of moving. (adjective)

> When the *hostile* aircraft flew overhead, they knew that the enemy was closing in. (adjective)

Other words in the same **word family** are:

- hostility (**noun**)
- hostilities (**plural noun**).

> From her angry expression I could sense her *hostility*. (noun)

> No one expected any trouble but *hostilities* broke out at midnight. (plural noun)

Word knowledge

'Hostile' comes from the Latin word *hostilis*, meaning 'enemy' or 'stranger'.

How does this information add to your understanding of the word 'hostile'?

Have your say

How might we know someone was feeling hostile? Describe the following features of someone showing hostility:

- facial expressions
- body language
- tone of voice.

Activity 1   Understanding the meaning

Using the information above, complete the following grid with more information about the word 'hostile'. Some ideas have been added to help you.

Definition
What does the word hostile mean?

Characteristics
What does hostile behaviour look like?
- An unfriendly facial expression – maybe with arms crossed

Hostile

Examples
Where might someone see a hostile person?
- When rival football teams play, the fans might be hostile.

Non-examples
What isn't hostile behaviour?
- Being friendly

Hostile 2

✏️ Activity 2 Exploring the meaning

Look at the word web of **synonyms** for the adjective 'hostile'. Use the word list on pages 76–78 to look up any unfamiliar words.

Word web: **hostile** — contrary, unwelcoming, antagonistic, malicious, combative

1) Match each synonym to a situation described below.

   a) how a parent reacts when you bring home a friend that they do not like
   ----

   b) a child who likes to do the opposite of what they are supposed to
   ----

   c) a politician who is always criticising people they disagree with, and causing offence
   ----

   d) someone who likes a challenge and competition
   ----

   e) a person who intends to harm others
   ----

2) Choose one of the synonyms and write a sentence using that word.

✏️ Activity 3 'Hostile' in context: reading skills

Read the extract below from *Where the World Ends* by Geraldine McCaughrean.
Quilliam is taking a boat across the sea to reach the Warrior Stac: a huge hostile rock.

> Even the sea was hostile to witchy Quilliam: the waves hissed. The temperature plummeted. The rain **doused** the embers of anger scorching Quill's guts, but he was not grateful: Rage was all that had been keeping him going.
>
> By the time he found Lower Bothy, his flesh was jumping with cold. Dead red jellyfish lay rotting in a row across the doorway: his particular horror come to greet him. Theirs was the only colour anywhere, in any direction, as far as the edge of the world.
>
> **doused** – drenched

1) Describe the sea in this extract.

   ----

2) Circle five words that suggest a hostile atmosphere and note down how they add to the overall **mood**/feeling of the extract.

25

Chapter 2: Mood and tone

3 Melancholy

The word 'melancholy' can be used as a **noun** or an **adjective**.

1) The noun 'melancholy' means a deep sadness.
2) The adjective 'melancholy' means sad and gloomy.

> The slow song was full of sadness and *melancholy*. (noun)

> Standing beside the grave, their *melancholy* eyes blurred with tears. (adjective)

Other words in the same **word family** are:

- melancholic (**adjective**)
- melancholically (**adverb**).

> She led a lonely, *melancholic* life. (adjective)

> The painting reflected a *melancholically* beautiful world. (adverb)

Word knowledge

The word 'melancholy' is linked to the Greek word *melas*, meaning 'black'.

How does this help your understanding of the word 'melancholy'?

 Have your say

What other colours are linked to specific emotions or moods?

Activity 1 — Understanding the meaning

1) Read the sentences below and tick those where forms of the word 'melancholy' are used correctly.

The only sounds were the distant, melancholy cries of a buzzard.	
She laughed with melancholy at the sight of her new puppy.	
Wind whistled melancholically through the old farmhouse walls.	
When the referee blew the final whistle, the whole town heard their loud, melancholy cheering.	
Despite the melancholy occasion, it was good to see all the family gathered together again.	

2) Rewrite an incorrect sentence, replacing the form of the word 'melancholy' with a more suitable alternative.

Melancholy 3

Activity 2 Exploring the meaning

Look at the word web of **synonyms** for the adjective 'melancholy'. Use the word list on pages 76–78 to look up any unfamiliar words.

1) All the synonyms are similar to the word 'melancholy', but they also have slightly different **connotations**. Read the definitions below and decide which links best with each synonym.

a) deep in thought

b) cannot be comforted by anything

c) showing grief because of loss

d) looking downwards, depressed

e) moody and gloomy

Word web: melancholy — pensive, disconsolate, glum, mournful, downcast

2) Think of two **antonyms** for the word 'melancholy'. Write them down and write your own definition for each of them.

Activity 3 'Melancholy' in context: reading skills

Read the extract below from *A Christmas Carol* by Charles Dickens. In this extract, the old man, Scrooge, is taken back in time to visit the school he went to as a child.

> They went, the Ghost and Scrooge, across the hall, to a door at the back of the house. It opened before them, and disclosed a long, bare, melancholy room, made barer still by lines of **plain deal forms** and desks. At one of these a lonely boy was reading near a feeble fire; and Scrooge sat down upon a form, and wept to see his poor forgotten self as he used to be.
>
> **plain deal forms** – long wooden benches

1) List three things about the **setting** that feel melancholy.

2) Why might someone feel melancholy when thinking about some time in their past?

27

Chapter 2: Mood and tone

4 Bleak

The **adjective** 'bleak' has two meanings:

1) cold, empty and unwelcoming
2) not at all hopeful.

> In Victorian times, housing conditions were *bleak* for many poor families who couldn't afford to heat or light their homes. (adjective)

> The future of his company looked *bleak*; his sales had been falling every year. (adjective)

Other words in the same **word family** are:

- bleakness (**noun**)
- bleakly (**adverb**).

> The *bleakness* of living in a lighthouse had never appealed to her; it was a cold and lonely life. (noun)

> His room was small, *bleakly* lit and never felt like home. (adverb)

The **bleakness** of living in a lighthouse had never appealed to her; it was a cold and lonely life.

💬 Have your say

What does a bleak setting look like? Describe the bleak features of the following places:

- multistorey car park
- mountains
- train station
- caves.

✏️ Activity 1   Understanding the meaning

1) Complete the sentences below by adding the correct form of the word 'bleak'.

   a) From the top deck of the bus I glimpsed their _____ and lonely faces.

   b) The streetlights flickered _____ , casting black shadows on the pavement.

   c) I closed my eyes as the train hurried through the _____ of the dark tunnel.

   d) The rain continued to fall on the _____ and gloomy moorland.

2) Write your own sentence using the word 'bleak'.

28

Bleak 4

✏️ Activity 2 Exploring the meaning

Look at the word web of **synonyms** for the adjective 'bleak'. Use the word list on pages 76–78 to look up any unfamiliar words.

Word web synonyms for **bleak**: exposed, barren, austere, dreary, empty, cheerless

1) Do the synonyms describe a landscape or a room? Add the words to the table below. If you think the word describes both a landscape and a room, you can add it to both columns.

Landscape	Room

2) Write a description of either a landscape or a room. Use some of the synonyms from the table in your description.

✏️ Activity 3 'Bleak' in context: reading skills

Read the extract below from an article about the moon landing. When astronauts landed on the Moon, they were the first people ever to see planet Earth 'rise' above the Moon's surface. It was a magical moment.

> They quickly scrambled for a camera – the first couple of images of 'Earthrise' were in black and white, **subsequent** photos were taken in colour. It is these colour photographs that became the **iconic** images of the environmental movement.
>
> They showed the stark contrast between the grey, desolate landscape of the lifeless Moon and the vivid blue-and-white orb of the **fertile** Earth – a symbol of warmth and life in a bleak desert of deathly coldness.
>
> **subsequent** – coming after
> **iconic** – famous, symbolic, representing an idea or belief
> **fertile** – able to produce crops

1) What is the 'bleak desert' that the writer compares with the colourful Earth?

----

2) Circle three other words in the extract that support the idea of the Moon being bleak.

3) What contrasting images do the words 'fertile' and 'deathly' create in the reader's mind?

29

Chapter 2: Mood and tone

5 Apprehensive

The **adjective** 'apprehensive' means worried or scared that something bad will happen.

> Although I've been working hard, I'm still *apprehensive* about the exam. (adjective)

Other words in the same **word family** are:

- apprehension (**noun**)
- apprehensively (**adverb**).

> It is perfectly normal to feel some *apprehension* when moving to a new school. (noun)

> Hearing an unknown noise, he glanced at the door *apprehensively*. (adverb)

Tip

The 'Have your say' task is asking you to use empathy – putting yourself in someone else's shoes to imagine how something feels for them. Think about an apprehensive moment from a film, book or your own experiences to help you empathise and justify your ideas.

Have your say

1) What age group might feel the most apprehensive and why?
2) What are the situations that might create apprehension for this age group?
3) How can we help someone who feels apprehensive?

✏ Activity 1 Understanding the meaning

Using the information above, complete the following grid with more information about the word 'apprehensive'. Some ideas have been added to help you.

Definition What does the word apprehensive mean?	**Characteristics** What does apprehensive behaviour look like? • Being unable to sit still
Examples When might someone feel apprehensive? • Going somewhere for the first time	**Non-examples** What isn't apprehensive behaviour? • Feeling relaxed

Apprehensive

30

Apprehensive 5

Activity 2 Exploring the meaning

Look at the word web of **synonyms** for the adjective 'apprehensive'. Use the word list on pages 76–78 to look up any unfamiliar words.

Word web synonyms for **apprehensive**: concerned, nervous, jittery, afraid, fearful, uneasy.

1) Choose three of the synonyms and add them to the table below. Think of a situation when this feeling might occur and write a sentence using the word correctly. An example has been done for you.

jittery	Since the accident, Frank felt jittery every time he heard a motorbike.

2) Now look closely at the definition of 'concerned': **feeling uncertain or unsure about something**
Explain how this word differs from 'apprehensive'.

Activity 3 'Apprehensive' in context: writing skills

On separate paper and using the ideas and words that you have explored, write a 50-word description of one of the following situations where you might feel apprehensive:

- the first training session when you have joined a new sports team
- presenting something to the whole class in a History lesson
- waiting to hear how your new puppy is after an operation.

Chapter 2: Mood and tone

6 Sinister

The **adjective** 'sinister' has two meanings:

1) looking or seeming evil or harmful
2) wicked or intending to do harm.

There was a moment of *sinister* silence before the bomb exploded. (adjective)

It was clear from her smirk that she had a *sinister* plan. (adjective)

Other words in the same **word family** are:

- sinisterness (**noun**)
- sinisterly (**adverb**).

The castle dungeon had an air of *sinisterness*. (noun)

Sliding *sinisterly* toward the mouse, the snake opened his jaws wide. (adverb)

The castle dungeon had an air of **sinisterness**.

Word knowledge

The word 'sinister' is linked to the Latin word *sinister* and the Old French *sinistre* meaning 'left'. It had **connotations** of being unlucky.

How does this help your understanding of the word 'sinister'?

💬 Have your say

Think about a sinister film or TV series you know. How do the following features help create the sinister atmosphere?

- Music
- Setting
- Weather
- Lighting

✏️ Activity 1 — Understanding the meaning

1) Read the sentences below and tick those where the word 'sinister' is used correctly.

Sunlight flooded the room, comforting him with a warm, sinister light.	
Her sinister laugh cut through the silence, terrifying us all.	
There was something sinister in the way the ship left the port after dark.	
Calmly, the athlete took his sinister position on the starting line.	

2) Rewrite an incorrect sentence, replacing the word 'sinister' with a more suitable alternative.

32

Sinister 6

✏ Activity 2 Exploring the meaning

Look at the word web of **synonyms** for the adjective 'sinister'. Use the word list on pages 76–78 to look up any unfamiliar words.

1) Look at the sinister settings in the table below. Using the synonyms from the word web, describe their appearance. The first has been done for you.

isolated farmhouse	The small yet intimidating farmhouse sat quiet and alone in acres of menacing moorland.
ruined castle	
abandoned ship	

2) Write a sentence describing a sinister character. Use the synonyms from the word web in your description.

✏ Activity 3 'Sinister' in context: reading skills

Read the extract below from *Room 13* by Robert Swindells. In this story, a school trip goes horribly wrong. Before leaving home, Fliss has a nightmare about the hotel in which she and her classmates are going to stay.

> The door closed silently behind her. Moonlight shone coldly through a stained-glass panel into a gloomy hallway. At the far end were stairs that went up into blackness. She didn't want to climb that stairway but her feet drew her along the hallway and up.
>
> She came to a landing with doors. The stairs took a turn and went on up. As Fliss climbed, it grew colder. There was another landing, more doors and another turn in the stair. ... She was at the top of the house. There were four doors, each with a number. 10. 11. 12. 13. As she read the numbers, door thirteen swung inward with a squeal. "No!" she whispered, but it was no use. Her feet carried her over the threshold …

1) Circle three words or phrases that create a sinister atmosphere in this extract.
2) On separate paper, explain how the writer has created a sinister atmosphere in this nightmare.

Tip

Think about the dark, the temperature, the sounds, Fliss's own fears and the connotations of number 13.

33

Chapter 2: Mood and tone

7 Incredulous

The **adjective** 'incredulous' means finding it difficult to believe something or being doubtful that something is true.

The driving instructor was *incredulous* that his student had passed. (adjective)

Other words in the same **word family** are:

- incredulity (**noun**)
- incredulously (**adverb**).

She stared at him with *incredulity* when he told her the truth. (noun)

"They gave *you* the job?" he muttered *incredulously*. (adverb)

Word knowledge

The word 'incredulous' is linked to the Latin word *credulus* meaning 'believing' or 'trusting'. The **prefix** 'in-' means 'not'.

How does this help your understanding of the word 'incredulous'?

💬 Have your say

Imagine that a family member is incredulous that you have now grown taller than them. How might you know they are feeling incredulous? Describe their body language and their word choices.

✏️ Activity 1 Understanding the meaning

Using the information above, complete the following grid with more information about the word 'incredulous'. Some ideas have been added to help you.

Definition	Characteristics
What does the word incredulous mean?	What does incredulous behaviour look like? • Silently staring at something
Examples	**Non-examples**
When might someone feel incredulous? • Getting top marks for something when you thought you had done badly	What isn't incredulous behaviour? • Being sure of something

Incredulous

Incredulous 7

✏️ Activity 2 — Exploring the meaning

1) The prefix 'in-' means 'not'. Here are some more words that include the prefix 'in-'. Write their definitions, then check them using a dictionary.

   a) incredible ………………………………………………………………………………

   b) incomplete ………………………………………………………………………………

   c) inadequate ………………………………………………………………………………

2) Write down more words that use the prefix 'in-' to turn a **root word** into its **antonym**. Here are a few to get you started.

   | inaction | inability | inconsiderate | in _____ | in _____ | in _____ |

3) a) Think of two **synonyms** for the word 'incredulous'.

   ………………………………………………………   ………………………………………………………

   b) Write two sentences, each including one of these words.

   ……

   ……

✏️ Activity 3 — 'Incredulous' in context: reading skills

In reviews, people give their opinion about films, books, shows or other performances. The extract below is from a review of a people's circus that tours all over the world.

> The evening was a rollercoaster of entertainment, transporting us through laughter, tears, astonishment, nail-biting horror, and the pure joy of music and dance. The colour, sparkle and imagination that went into the staging and costumes was completely spellbinding. But within the magical atmosphere were astounding physical **feats**. The acrobatics and daredevil **aerial** performances left the audience incredulous — and hardly daring to breathe. The thunderous applause when the performers were safely on the ground again was a **tsunami** of relief.
>
> **feats** – brave achievements
> **aerial** – taking place in the air
> **tsunami** – a huge sea wave

1) Explain why you think the audience was incredulous.

   ……

2) Why does the reviewer compare the applause to a 'tsunami'? Explain what this shows about the **mood** and **tone** of the evening.

   ……

   ……

3) On separate paper, describe a performance you have seen that left you incredulous. It could be linked to sport, music, dance or any other performance.

35

Chapter 2: Mood and tone

 Elated

The **adjective** 'elated' means feeling very pleased and excited.

> We were *elated* to announce the birth of the panda cubs. (adjective)

Other words in the same **word family** are:
- elation (**noun**)
- elate (**verb**)
- elatedly (**adverb**).

> Smiling in *elation*, the students shared their amazing exam results. (noun)

> The beautiful scenery at the resort will *elate* you. (verb)

> The delighted audience clapped and cheer *elatedly*. (adverb)

We were **elated** to announce the birth of the panda cubs.

Have your say

In which of the following moments would you feel the most elated? Rank them and give reasons for your answers.
- Being chosen to represent your country in the Olympics
- Achieving top grades in all your exams
- Winning the lottery
- Getting a million followers online

Word knowledge

The word 'elated' is linked to the Latin word *elatus* meaning 'raised'.

How does this help your understanding of the word 'elated'?

Activity 1 — Understanding the meaning

1) Complete the sentences below by adding the correct form of the word 'elated'.

   a) Waving _____, she raced from the car.

   b) Laughing in _____, the friends left the cinema.

   c) _____, the accountant left the office for the last time.

   d) The travellers were _____ to be upgraded to first class.

2) Write two sentences of your own using the word 'elated'.

Elated 8

Activity 2 — Exploring the meaning

Look at the word web of **synonyms** for the adjective 'elated'. Use the word list on pages 76–78 to look up any unfamiliar words.

1) Add three more synonyms to the word web.

2) Choose one of the synonyms and write a sentence using that word.

3) Look at the words below and decide which is the best **antonym** for 'elated'. Give reasons for your answer.

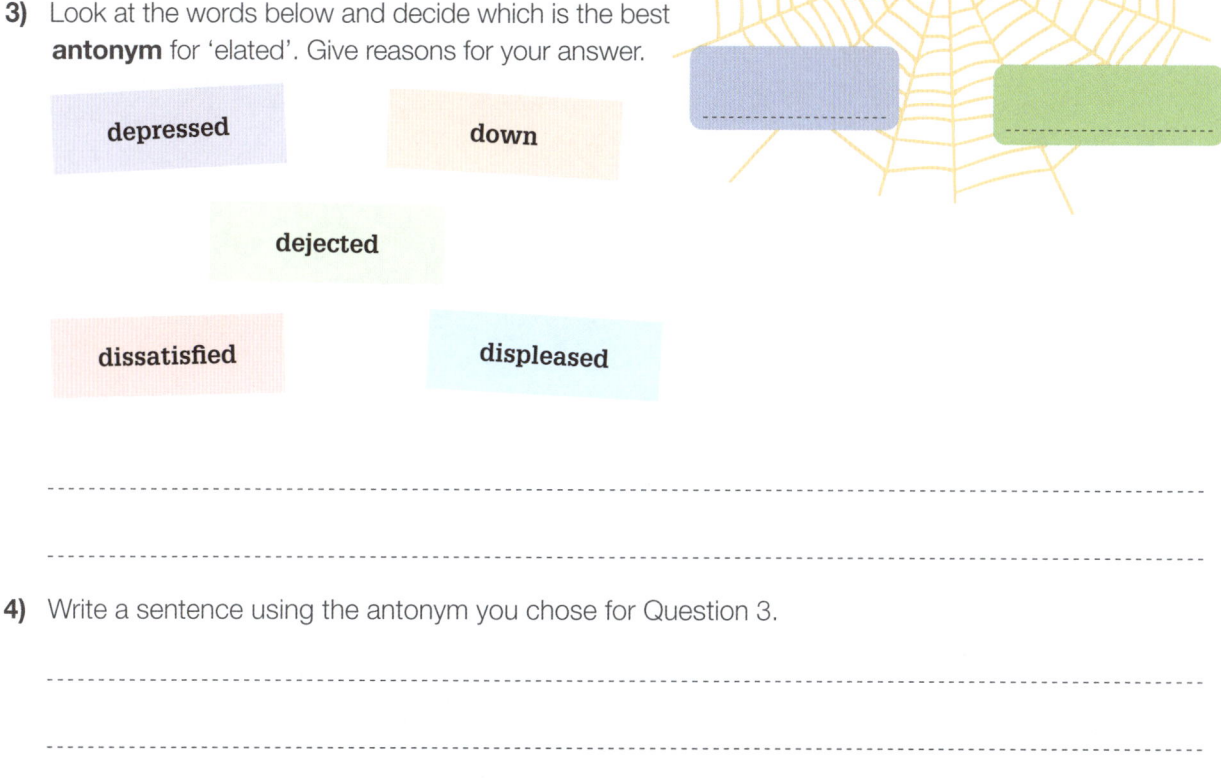

- depressed
- down
- dejected
- dissatisfied
- displeased

Word web contains: exhilarated, euphoric, elated (centre)

_____

_____

4) Write a sentence using the antonym you chose for Question 3.

_____

_____

Activity 3 — 'Elated' in context: writing skills

Imagine a school election for either head boy or head girl has taken place. All the votes have been counted and the results are in. The two candidates have very different feelings. Both candidates address their classmates and describe how they feel. On separate paper, complete their speeches using the sentence starters below. Both candidates should show respect for each other and each other's views.

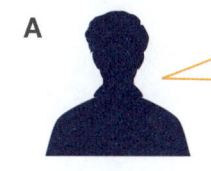

A: I feel absolutely elated because …

B: I must admit I am disappointed because …

37

Chapter 2: Mood and tone

9 Foreboding

The word 'foreboding' can be used as a **noun** or an **adjective**.

1) The noun 'foreboding' means a feeling that trouble is coming.
2) The adjective 'foreboding' suggests that something bad is going to happen.

> He felt a sense of *foreboding* as he opened the exam paper. (noun)

> The dark, empty car park's *foreboding* appearance worried us all. (adjective)

Another word in the same **word family** is the **verb** 'forbode'.

> The dark, gathering clouds *forbode* a terrible storm. (verb)

Word knowledge

The word 'foreboding' contains the **prefix** 'fore-' meaning 'before' or 'in front of'.

How does this help your understanding of the word 'foreboding'?

💬 Have your say

"Childhood has no forebodings."

– George Eliot (author)

1) What do you think the quotation above means?
2) Do you agree or disagree? Justify your ideas with examples to support your points.

✏️ Activity 1 — Understanding the meaning

1) Read the following foreboding situations and note down the picture they create for you. The first has been done for you.

Situation	Picture created
A foreboding pack of dogs	snarling, fierce-looking dogs who are staring at me
A foreboding doorway	
Foreboding weather	
Her foreboding stare	

2) On separate paper, choose one of the images above and bring to life what you see in a 50-word description.

Foreboding 9

✏️ Activity 2 Exploring the meaning

The prefix 'fore-' can be added to many words to mean 'before' or 'in front of'. Look at the words on the tree branches that start with the prefix 'fore-'. Use the word list on pages 76–78 to look up any unfamiliar words.

forewarn __
foresee __
forecast __
foreground __
foreshadow __
foreward __

1) Read the definitions below and decide which links best with each word.

a) the part of a scene or picture that is closest to the person looking at it

b) to be aware of something before it happens

c) to make a prediction about what is likely to happen, for example about the weather

d) to alert someone about something so they can take action

e) a short introduction at the beginning of a book

f) to be a sign of something that is likely to happen, for example in a story

2) Choose one of the words. Write a sentence including that word. Try to show the exact meaning of the word in your sentence.

✏️ Activity 3 'Foreboding' in context: writing skills

Imagine that you have spent the last month on a mission to explore the possibility of life on Mars. You have discovered signs that suggest you are being watched by something or someone.

On separate paper, write a space log for Mission Control, recording your fears that you are not alone. The overall **tone** of the letter should be one of foreboding. If possible, use the words from Activity 2, such as 'foresee' and 'forewarn'.

> Space log No. 48
> During the last three days of this mission, there have been signs that lead me to conclude that someone – or something – is watching our every move. I first became concerned when …

Tip

Think about how you would feel writing the update. Which words can you use to get your feelings across?

39

Chapter 3: Individual and society

1 Moral

The **adjective** 'moral' has two meanings:
1) what you believe is right or wrong behaviour
2) good, following the accepted rules of behaviour.

> It was her *moral* duty to tell the police about the crime. (adjective)

> He is a decent, *moral* leader, who makes decisions for the good of the whole group. (adjective)

Other words in the same **word family** are:
- moral (**noun**)
- morality (**noun**)
- morally (**adverb**).

> The *moral* of the story is to be kind to others. (noun)

> We continue to debate the *morality* of fox hunting. (noun)

> At what age is it *morally* right to leave a child alone? (adverb)

Word knowledge

If a person is 'immoral' they behave in a way that goes against the accepted rules of behaviour.

The **prefix** 'im-' can turn a **root word** into meaning the opposite. What other words begin with the prefix 'im-'?

💬 Have your say

Which of these morals do you think is the most important? Rank them and give reasons for your answers.

- Taking responsibility for helping out at home
- Being loyal to your friends
- Respecting your teachers
- Being tolerant of other people's views

✏️ Activity 1 — Understanding the meaning

1) Read the sentences below and tick those where the word 'moral' is used correctly.

They have a moral obligation to pay what they owe.	
With a sad and moral sigh, he drove the car away.	
His moral code kept him on the right path.	
Frightened and moral, the sparrows flew into the hedge.	

2) Rewrite an incorrect sentence, replacing the word 'moral' with a more suitable alternative.

Moral

✏️ Activity 2 — Exploring the meaning

A moral dilemma is a situation where you have to make a difficult choice between two actions.

1) Read the following moral dilemma and fill in the table with your ideas about the two conflicting sides to the dilemma.

> Your best friend has shared something on social media that has upset a lot of students at your school. The headteacher has asked for information about the post and you know that it was your friend who posted it. Should you betray your friend or lie to the headteacher?

Reasons to tell the truth	Reasons to lie

2) In no more than 25 words, describe what is so difficult about a moral dilemma.

✏️ Activity 3 — 'Moral' in context: reading skills

Read the extract below from an article where writer David Walliams talks about why young people are so delighted by Roald Dahl's stories. He is talking in particular about the book *George's Marvellous Medicine*.

> In his story, George effectively kills his grandmother. She is certainly dead at the end of the book. This lack of **conventional** morality is extremely **compelling** for young readers, who feel as though they are entering a thrillingly dangerous world.
>
> **conventional** – ordinary   **compelling** – fascinating

1) How might someone act if they have a 'lack of conventional morality'?

----

2) What would 'conventional morality' say about George killing his grandmother? Would it be right or wrong? Explain why.

----

3) In your own words, explain why young readers find this lack of 'conventional morality' exciting in Roald Dahl's novels.

Chapter 3: Individual and society

2 Virtuous

The **adjective** 'virtuous' means behaving in a morally good way.

> She was a *virtuous* employee; she followed all of the company rules. (adjective)

Other words in the same **word family** are:

- virtue (**noun**)
- virtuously (**adverb**).

> Patience is a *virtue*. (noun)

> Turning the vacuum cleaner off, he smiled *virtuously* at his tidy, clean house. (adverb)

Word knowledge

'Virtuous' comes from the Latin word *virtus*, meaning 'moral strength' or 'high character'. It also refers to courage and bravery in war.

How does this information add to your understanding of the word 'virtuous'?

💬 Have your say

"It makes you feel very virtuous when you forgive people."

– Lucy M. Montgomery (author)

1) What do you think the quotation above means?
2) Do you agree or disagree? Justify your ideas with examples to support your points.

✎ Activity 1 — Understanding the meaning

Using the information above, complete the following grid with more information about the word 'virtuous'. Some ideas have been added to help you.

Definition	Characteristics
What does the word virtuous mean?	What does virtuous behaviour look like?
	• Being a morally good person

Virtuous

Examples	Non-examples
When might someone feel virtuous?	What isn't virtuous behaviour?
• Helping others	• Not following morals

42

Virtuous 2

Activity 2 — Exploring the meaning

Look at the word web of **synonyms** for the adjective 'virtuous'. Use the word list on pages 76–78 to look up any unfamiliar words.

Word web: **virtuous** — honourable, exemplary, ethical, principled, worthy, blameless

1) Circle the word that you think best describes someone who is a good role model for others to follow. Explain the reason for your choice.

   ----

2) Name someone who you would describe as 'virtuous'. He or she could be a character from a book, film or TV series, or someone from real life. Explain what virtues they have shown.

Activity 3 — 'Virtuous' in context: reading skills

Read the extract below from *The Strange Case of Dr Jekyll and Mr Hyde* by Robert Louis Stevenson. In this extract, Dr Jekyll explains how his personality became split into two characters: one good, one bad. While his virtuous character rested, his bad character took control and acted as if it were a separate person completely.

> At that time my virtue **slumbered**; my evil, kept awake by ambition, was alert and swift to seize the occasion; and the thing that was **projected** was Edward Hyde.

slumbered – slept   **projected** – created

1) Look at the title of the story. How do you think this extract links to this title?

   ----

2) If you were writing this story, what sort of virtues would you give Dr Jekyll?

   ----

3) What sort of vices would you give to Mr Hyde?

Tip

A 'virtue' is a good quality or strength in someone's character.

A 'vice' is a weak quality or fault in someone's character.

Think about virtues and vices that would be an interesting contrast in one person. How might they develop the **plot** and drama of the story?

Chapter 3: Individual and society

3 Sentiment

The **noun** 'sentiment' has two meanings:

1) an opinion or attitude that you have about something
2) a show of feeling or emotion.

> I understand your *sentiments*, but I don't feel the same way. (noun)

> She kept the letters out of *sentiment* for the summer they shared. (noun)

Other words in the same **word family** are:

- sentimental (**adjective**)
- sentimentality (**noun**)
- sentimentally (**adverb**).

> He was very *sentimental* and loved his pets very much. (adjective)

> A wave of *sentimentality* put a tear in Grandma's eye as she looked through the old photographs. (noun)

> Spending your time looking *sentimentally* at the past could stop you enjoying the present. (adverb)

Activity 1 — Understanding the meaning

1) Complete the sentences below by adding the correct form of the word 'sentiment'.

   a) He had no _____ about his childhood home.

   b) I shared this _____ several times but no one seemed to hear.

   c) The _____ film made us all cry.

   d) _____, I cuddled the teddy bear my older sister had given me.

2) Write your own sentence using the word 'sentiment'.

   _____

   _____

Word knowledge

'Sentiment' comes from the Latin word *sentire* meaning 'to feel or sense'.

How does this information add to your understanding of the word 'sentiment'?

Tip

There can be a slightly negative side to the word 'sentimental' – putting too much importance on emotions, especially love or sadness, to the point that you appear foolish.

Have your say

"All the beautiful sentiments in the world weigh less than a single, lovely action."

– James Russell Lowell (poet)

1) What do you think the quotation above means?

2) Do you agree or disagree? Justify your ideas with examples to support your points.

Sentiment 3

✏️ Activity 2 — Exploring the meaning

Look at the word web of **synonyms** for the noun 'sentiment'. Use the word list on pages 76–78 to look up any unfamiliar words.

1) Write two sentences, including one of the synonyms in each. Try to show the meaning of the words in each.

Word web for **sentiment**: belief, feeling, thought, opinion, view, attitude.

2) Add more synonyms to the word web for 'sentimental'.

Word web for **sentimental**: emotional, nostalgic, loving.

3) Write two sentences. One should include the word 'sentimental' and the other should include one of the synonyms.

✏️ Activity 3 — 'Sentiment' in context: writing skills

Imagine you are an elderly person writing a diary. Today you visited the ruins of your childhood home. On separate paper, complete the diary entry. Remember to write your diary entry in the **first person**, using **pronouns** such as 'I' and 'we', and the **past tense**.

> Sunday 7th July
> Visiting the old house triggered a flood of memories. I was overwhelmed by the different sentiments that swept over me ...

45

Chapter 3: Individual and society

4 Civilised

The **adjective** 'civilised' has two meanings:
1) polite and well-mannered
2) having a well-developed culture and society.

> We would like your child to behave in a *civilised* way; he must not stand on the seats. (adjective)

> The Incan Empire was a *civilised* society that transformed villages into large cities. (adjective)

Other words in the same **word family** are:

- civilisation (**noun**)
- civil (**adjective**).

> After months of living isolated and alone, she was back in *civilisation*. (noun)

> She was *civil* to her but they were no longer friends. (adjective)

Word knowledge

'Civilised' comes from the Latin word *civilis* meaning 'good citizen'. A citizen is a person who belongs to a particular city or country. To be 'civil' literally means to be 'someone who fulfils the duty of a citizen'.

How does this information add to your understanding of the word 'civilised'?

💬 Have your say

1) What do you think the duties of a citizen might be? List your top five ideas.
2) Do you think the duties of a citizen have changed with the passing of time?

✏️ Activity 1 — Understanding the meaning

1) Complete the sentences below by adding the correct form of the word 'civilised'.

   a) Only _____ behaviour at the table, please!

   b) The people of the Ancient Egyptian _____ believed in more than 2000 gods.

   c) Hundreds of miles from _____, the explorers began to fear the worst.

   d) It's important to discuss these things in a _____ manner.

2) Write your own sentences using the words 'civilised' and 'civilisation'.

Civilised 4

Activity 2 — Exploring the meaning

Look at the word web of **synonyms** for the adjective 'civilised'.

Word web: **civilised** — polite, educated, humane, sophisticated, cultured, tolerant

1) All the synonyms are similar to the word 'civilised', but they also have slightly different **connotations**. Read the descriptions below and decide which links best with each synonym. Use the word list on pages 76–78 to help you.

a) enjoy art, literature and music
_____

b) show respect and good manners
_____

c) accept different viewpoints even if you don't agree with them
_____

d) show kindness or forgiveness
_____

e) have experience of the world
_____

f) trained to gain knowledge and learn skills
_____

2) Think of two **antonyms** for the word 'civilised'. Write them down and write your own definition for each of them.

_____
_____
_____
_____
_____
_____

Activity 3 — 'Civilised' in context: writing skills

Imagine that you are on the school council and a group of students have been behaving badly. On separate paper, create a leaflet or a poster about civilised behaviour in school to give advice to other students. You could think about how to show respect for each other, teachers and visitors.

Chapter 3: Individual and society

5 Prejudice

The word 'prejudice' can be used as a **noun** or a **verb**.

1) The noun 'prejudice' means a strong unreasonable feeling of not liking or trusting someone.
2) The verb 'prejudice' means to cause harm from an action or decision.

> His obvious *prejudice* against young people was clear from the way he refused to listen to them. (noun)

> If you fail to improve the school, you *prejudice* the students' education. (verb)

Other words in the same **word family** are:

- prejudiced (**adjective**)
- prejudicially (**adverb**).

> The court case was *prejudiced* from the start; one of the witnesses knew the accused. (adjective)

> The headteacher made it clear to students that behaving *prejudicially* toward others would not be accepted. (adverb)

Word knowledge

The word 'prejudice' comes from the Latin word *praeiudicium* meaning 'prior judgment'. The **prefix** *prae-* means 'before' and *iudicium* means 'judgement'.

How does this information add to your understanding of the word 'prejudice'?

💬 Have your say

1) Do you think society and the media label teenagers in a prejudiced way? Why?
2) How could we change the prejudiced ideas some people hold about teenagers?

✏️ Activity 1 — Understanding the meaning

1) Read the sentences below and tick those where forms of the word 'prejudice' are used correctly.

The fact that you don't like her is just simple prejudice.	
He was hungry and fed up as he prejudiced a place to park.	
Don't pretend that there isn't some prejudice behind this decision.	
There is always next time he thought, moving prejudicially away.	

2) Rewrite an incorrect sentence, replacing the form of the word 'prejudice' with a more suitable alternative.

48

Prejudice 5

✏️ Activity 2 — Exploring the meaning

Look at the word web of **synonyms** for the noun 'prejudice'. Use the word list on pages 76–78 to look up any unfamiliar words.

1) Circle the synonym that sounds least serious. Explain your answer.

   ----

2) Underline the synonym that sounds most serious. Explain your answer.

Word web synonyms: bias, narrow-mindedness, bigotry, preconception, discrimination — prejudice

3) Write down two **antonyms** for 'prejudice'.

✏️ Activity 3 — 'Prejudice' in context: reading skills

In 2014, actor Emma Watson called on men and boys to support the global campaign HeForShe, for gender equality. In this speech, she explains that real gender equality will be good for both women and men.

> HeForShe is about freedom. I want men to take up this **mantle**. So their daughters, sisters and mothers can be free from prejudice but also so that their sons have permission to be **vulnerable** and human too – **reclaim** those parts of themselves they abandoned and in doing so be a more true and complete version of themselves.
>
> **mantle** – cause
> **vulnerable** – able to be emotionally open
> **reclaim** – take back

1) In your own words, explain what the campaign HeForShe is about.

   ----

2) What do you understand by the phrase 'free from prejudice'?

   ----

3) How does Emma Watson believe boys may benefit from gender equality?

Chapter 3: Individual and society

6 Benevolent

The **adjective** 'benevolent' has two meanings:

1) someone kind and helpful, who wishes to do good for others
2) created for a charitable purpose.

> She was a *benevolent* lady, always helping other people. (adjective)

> The *benevolent* fund paid for things like house repairs. (adjective)

Other words in the same **word family** are:

- benevolence (**noun**)
- benevolently (**adverb**).

> We were grateful for the *benevolence* shown to the tired, hungry refugees. (noun)

> Smiling *benevolently*, they gave up their seats for the elderly couple. (adverb)

*Smiling **benevolently**, they gave up their seats for the elderly couple.*

Have your say

What sort of benevolent actions might you see in the following places?

- A foodbank
- A hospital
- A classroom

Activity 1 — Understanding the meaning

1) Complete the sentences below to show your understanding of the words 'benevolent', 'benevolence' and 'benevolently'.

   a) The teenagers acted benevolently when they _____.

   b) I gave the money to the benevolent fund, thinking _____.

   c) Her benevolence was shown by _____.

2) Now write your own sentence using the word 'benevolent'.

Benevolent 6

✏️ Activity 2 — Exploring the meaning

The Latin word *bene* means 'well' or 'good'. 'Bene-' is often found at the beginning of words that are linked to something positive.

1) Find three other words that start with 'bene-'. Write a definition for each of them and then check your definitions in a dictionary.

a) bene_____	--
b) bene_____	--
c) bene_____	--

2) Read the sentences below.

> The headteacher listened to the students' explanation and gave them the benefit of the doubt. They left unpunished, although I think they were guilty.

What does it mean to give someone 'the benefit of the doubt'?

✏️ Activity 3 — 'Benevolent' in context: reading skills

Douglas William Jerrold was an English writer who lived in the 19th century. He was famous for his wit and sense of humour. Read the quotation below.

> "He was so benevolent, so merciful a man that, in his mistaken passion, he would have held an umbrella over a duck in a shower of rain."

1) Why would it be strange to hold an umbrella over a duck?

----

2) In your own words, describe 'mistaken passion'.

----

3) How does the word 'benevolent' help your understanding of this quotation?

Chapter 3: Individual and society

7 Betray

The **verb** 'betray' has two meanings:

1) to break someone's trust
2) to reveal something without meaning to.

> I felt *betrayed* when you shared my secret. (verb)

> If she was sad about leaving, she did not *betray* her feelings. (verb)

Another word in the same **word family** is the **noun** 'betrayal'.

> The worst way to hurt a friend is the *betrayal* of their trust. (noun)

*If she was sad about leaving, she did not **betray** her feelings.*

💬 Have your say

"Betray a friend and you'll often find you have betrayed yourself."
— From *Aesop's Fables*

1) What do you think this quotation means?
2) Do you agree? Why/Why not?
3) Is it possible to betray yourself? How?
4) What are the consequences of betrayal?

Try to justify your ideas with examples to support your points.

✏️ Activity 1 — Understanding the meaning

1) Read the sentences below and tick those where forms of the word 'betray' are used correctly.

It was pure betrayal to leave him out of the group.	
Carefully betraying the car, I followed him down the road.	
They accused him of betraying his country during the war.	
Despite feeling upset, she didn't betray her emotions to anyone.	
Unlocking the door, she betrayed heavy footsteps behind her.	

2) Rewrite an incorrect sentence, replacing the form of the word 'betray' with a more suitable alternative.

Betray 7

✏ Activity 2 — Exploring the meaning

Look at the word web of **synonyms** for the verb 'betray'. Use the word list on pages 76–78 to look up any unfamiliar words.

Word web: **betray** — deceive, mislead, cheat, double-cross, trick

1) These synonyms have other **connotations**. Which word do you think is most likely to be associated with these situations?

   a) a magician's act ....

   b) lying to your family ....

   c) talking about a friend behind their back ....

   d) not being faithful in a relationship ....

   e) letting a parent believe you are doing homework when you are gaming ....

2) Complete this sentence.

   The most hurtful betrayal of all was ....

✏ Activity 3 — 'Betray' in context: reading skills

Read the extract below from *Scavengers* by Darren Simpson. Landfill lives alone with his guardian 'the scavenger' on a rubbish tip called Hinterland. When he tries to explore beyond Hinterland, the scavenger is furious and locks him out of their home, the Nook.

> The scavenger scratched beneath his hat and took a deep breath. His gaze was fixed ahead. "Landfill. I'm sorry about last night – about suspecting the worst. But I was so frightened. I was so scared of what'd happen to you."
>
> The boy's face darkened. "Then why'd you lock me out of the Nook?"
>
> "You know why. You broke rule twelve – went above the wall, into plain sight. Under Hunger's Eye too! You put all of Hinterland at risk. Can't you see what that looks like? Betrayal – that's what. I was so … disappointed. Heartbroken and angry."

1) How does the scavenger describe his feeling of betrayal?

   ....

2) What is the betrayal that has been committed?

   ....

3) On separate paper, explain how a betrayal might make you feel. Use about 30 words.

53

Chapter 3: Individual and society

8 Industrious

The **adjective** 'industrious' means hard-working.

> The people who are happy at work are the most *industrious*. (adjective)

Other words in the same **word family** are:

- industriousness (**noun**)
- industriously (**adverb**).

> I finished all my homework, in a flurry of *industriousness*. (noun)

> They worked *industriously* all day so they could celebrate in the evening. (adverb)

Word knowledge

The word 'industrious' comes from the Latin word *industria* meaning 'activity'.

How does this information add to your understanding of the word 'industrious'?

💬 Have your say

1) Discuss what being industrious might look like for the following people:
   - a teacher
   - a carer
   - a dog-walker
   - a newsreader
   - a builder.

2) How would you know if they were not being industrious?
   Try to justify your ideas with examples to support your points.

✏️ Activity 1 Understanding the meaning

Using the information above, complete the following grid with more information about the word 'industrious'. Some ideas have been added to help you.

Definition What does the word industrious mean?	**Characteristics** What does industrious behaviour look like? • Completing all your tasks
Examples When might someone feel industrious? • After cleaning their bedroom	**Non-examples** What isn't industrious behaviour? • Not handing in your homework

Industrious

Industrious 8

✏️ Activity 2   Exploring the meaning

Look at the word web of **synonyms** for the adjective 'industrious'. Use the word list on pages 76–78 to look up any unfamiliar words.

Synonyms: diligent, hard-working, focused, tireless, **industrious**, productive, conscientious

1) Describe a time that you have been industrious and what the outcome was.

   ....

   ....

2) Choose two synonyms for 'industrious' that you would like to see on your school report. Explain why you would like to be described like this.

   ....

   ....

   ....

   ....

3) Explain why it is good to be industrious.

   ....

   ....

✏️ Activity 3   'Industrious' in context: writing skills

Here are some **antonyms** for 'industrious'.

lazy   inactive   idle   lethargic   lax   dallying

On separate paper, write an email to a hotel to complain about your recent visit. You stayed there last year and the staff were helpful and industrious, but this year has been awful. Use the synonyms and antonyms above to help you. The opening has been started for you.

> Dear Hotel Splendid,
>
> We are so disappointed.
>
> We had a wonderful time in Bournemouth last year. However, this year we found…

Tip

To add strength to your complaint, compare how great your visit was last year with how awful it has been this year by using some of the following techniques:

- rhetorical questions
- direct address
- rule of three
- emotive language.

55

Chapter 3: Individual and society

9 Inferior

The word 'inferior' can be used as an **adjective** or a **noun**.

1) The adjective 'inferior' means less good or less important than someone or something else.
2) The noun 'inferior' means a person who is lower in position or rank than someone else.

> The fish we caught were *inferior* to our last catch. (adjective)

> She was a soldier; her captain's *inferior*. (noun)

Another word in the same **word family** is the noun 'inferiority'.

> Being around his successful older brother gave him a feeling of *inferiority*. (noun)

*The fish we caught were **inferior** to our last catch.*

💬 Have your say

"No one can make you feel inferior, without your consent."
— Eleanor Roosevelt (political figure)

'Consent' means allowing something to happen.

1) What does this quotation mean? Put it into your own words.
2) Do you agree with the quotation? Why/Why not?
   Try to justify your ideas with examples to support your points.

Word knowledge

'Inferior' comes from the Latin word *inferus* meaning 'low'. The **antonym** 'superior' comes from the Latin word *super* meaning 'above'.

How does this information add to your understanding of the word 'inferior'?

✏️ Activity 1 — Understanding the meaning

1) Look at the table below. Complete it with some ideas about why you might feel inferior to others in these situations. The first one has been done for you.

Situation	Why you might worry about being inferior
Waiting for an interview with other people	You might be feeling nervous and worried about being inferior if the other people seem to know more or have more experience than you.
Handing in a piece of really tricky homework	
Joining a new sports team	

2) Circle any three of the words you have used that most suggest a sense of inferiority.

Inferior 9

✏ Activity 2 Exploring the meaning

Look at the word web of **synonyms** for the adjective 'inferior'. Use the word list on pages 76–78 to look up any unfamiliar words.

Word web synonyms for **inferior**: imperfect, mediocre, inadequate, subordinate, junior, low-grade.

1) Divide the synonyms into two lists: words that are most likely to describe people and words that are most likely to describe things. Some words may belong in both lists.

People	Things

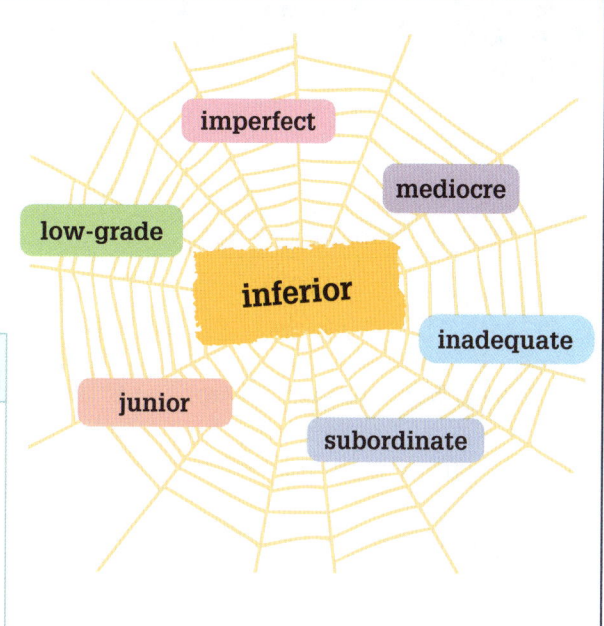

2) Choose one word from each list and write a sentence including it. Try to show the meaning of the word in each sentence.

3) Could the synonyms you have chosen be replaced by the word 'inferior' without changing the meaning of the sentences? Explain why or why not.

✏ Activity 3 'Inferior' in context: writing skills

On separate paper, write an advertisement for a product, such as a new brand of trainers. Use a persuasive **tone** to encourage people to buy this product. Use the words 'inferior' and 'superior' in your advertisement. Follow the steps below.

Step 1: Decide on a brand name, for example 'Supreme'.

Step 2: Explain why this brand is so good.

Step 3: Compare it to other brands and point out why they are all inferior.

Step 4: Think up a short, memorable slogan, for example 'Why settle for inferior when you can be Supreme?'

> **Tip**
>
> Remember that synonyms can have different **connotations**, so they do not always have the same meaning.

57

Chapter 4: Analysis and explanation

1 Observe

The **verb** 'observe' has three meanings:

1) to see and notice something
2) to make a comment
3) to take part in a tradition, religious festival or holiday, or follow a set of rules.

> Jake *observed* a look of terror on the child's face. (verb)

> "It's raining," she *observed*. (verb)

> We will *observe* a two-minute silence. (verb)

Other words in the same **word family** are:

- observation (**noun**)
- observational (**adjective**).

> Scientists have made several new *observations*. (noun)

> *Observational* comedy is about noticing things from everyday life. (adjective)

Have your say

Think of three things each of the following people might observe during their work:

- a taxi driver
- a lifeguard
- a headteacher
- a doctor.

Activity 1 Understanding the meaning

1) Read the examples below and add the letter you feel applies to the correct meaning of 'observe' from the three meanings below. The first has been done for you.

   a) to see and notice something
   b) to make a remark
   c) to take part in a custom, religious festival or holiday, or follow a set of rules.

Example	Letter
It's time to observe the two-minute silence.	c
This new observation changed the engineer's plans.	
She observed that it was nearly time for dinner so we all sat at the table.	
Have you observed how many people forget to wash their hands?	
"It's getting late," he observed.	
Could all guests observe the dress code for the wedding, please?	

2) Now write three sentences of your own, using the word 'observe' in a variety of ways.

58

Observe 1

Activity 2 — Exploring the meaning

1) Using the information on page 58, complete the following grid with more information about the word 'observe'. Some ideas have been added to help you.

Definition What does the word observe mean?	**Characteristics** What might someone do if they were observing? • Noting down what you see
Examples When might someone observe? • Looking for evidence	**Non-examples** What is an example of someone not observing? • Ignoring something

Observe

2) List four similar words or **synonyms** for 'observe'. The first has been done for you.

   a) watch
   b) _____
   c) _____
   d) _____

Activity 3 — 'Observe' in context: reading skills

Read the extract below from a newspaper article. A journalist was invited to see Britain's last tiger act with the Great British Circus. Although he had mixed feelings about animals performing in circuses, he felt that the tiger enjoyed doing the tricks for treats.

> It's hard to believe his [the owner's] circus-bred tigers have a harder life than the average housecat. They certainly have a more **stimulating** day than bored zoo animals, and a longer life than their endangered cousins in the wild.
>
> It felt like a **privilege** to observe such majestic creatures **at close quarters** and it was clearly an educational experience for the **enthralled** children in the ringside seats.
>
> **stimulating** – interesting
> **at close quarters** – close by
> **privilege** – special opportunity
> **enthralled** – fascinated

1) Why do you think the writer uses the word 'observe' rather than 'see' or 'look at'?

   _____
   _____
   _____

2) Explain why it is useful to observe things before making decisions and judgements.

   _____
   _____
   _____

59

Chapter 4: Analysis and explanation

2 Contrast

The word 'contrast' can be used as a **noun** or a **verb**.

1) The noun 'contrast' means a clear difference between things.
2) The verb 'contrast' means to compare things to show their clear differences.

> When I saw the brothers together, the *contrast* between them was surprising. (noun)

> When we *contrast* these colours, you can clearly see which is darker. (verb)

Other words in the same **word family** are:

- contrasting (**adjective**)
- contrastingly (**adverb**).

> There are two *contrasting* ways to look at the problem. (adjective)

> We sold out of cakes but, *contrastingly*, these biscuits did not sell at all. (adverb)

*When I saw the brothers together, the **contrast** between them was surprising.*

💬 Have your say

How many contrasts can you think of between the following pairs?

- Primary and secondary school
- Dogs and cats
- Holidays and birthdays
- Netflix and YouTube

✏️ Activity 1 — Understanding the meaning

1) Read the sentences below and tick those where forms of the word 'contrast' are used correctly.

The contrast in the sound of my new speaker is just amazing.	
Although we have contrasting ideas, it's important to listen to what everyone says.	
I met the identical twins and immediately saw the contrast in their looks.	
His polite speech contrasts with his terrible behaviour.	

2) Rewrite an incorrect sentence, replacing the form of the word 'contrast' with a more suitable alternative.

Contrast 2

✏️ Activity 2 — Exploring the meaning

1) Read these exam-style questions and note down what the task is asking for. The first one has been done for you.

Exam-style question	My own words
Describe the painting, in contrast to the photograph.	Looking closely at the painting, what differences are there between the painting and the photograph? What stands out most?
What contrasts can you make between the two characters?	
How might you contrast the two YouTubers?	

2) Write two of your own 'contrast' questions. You could use the ideas from the 'Have your say' box on page 60 to help you.

✏️ Activity 3 — 'Contrast' in context: writing skills

Imagine you are judging a painting competition. You have to choose a winner between the two seaside scenes below.

On separate paper, describe the two paintings, pointing out the contrasts between them. Think about the differences in colour, **mood**, detail and style. Remember to use comparison words and phrases.

Tip

When we contrast ideas, it helps to use comparison words and phrases such as: whereas, but, however, unlike, alternatively, otherwise, instead, conversely, on the other hand.

61

Chapter 4: Analysis and explanation

3 Characterise

The **verb** 'characterise' has two meanings:

1) to describe a person's character in a certain way
2) to be typical of something.

> Her friends *characterised* her as confident. (verb)

> The cold winds *characterised* the loneliness of the place. (verb)

Other words in the same **word family** are:

- characterisation (**noun**)
- characteristic (**adjective/noun**)
- characteristically (**adverb**).

> The film's *characterisation* of women annoyed many people. (noun)

> This type of flower is *characteristic* of this region. (adjective)

> Greed was the dog's main *characteristic*. (noun)

> His smile was *characteristically* warm and sunny. (adverb)

Word knowledge

'Characterise' comes from the Medieval Latin word *characterizare*, meaning 'to engrave a mark or symbol'.

How does the word 'engrave' add to your understanding of the word 'characterise'?

💬 Have your say

Imagine a very unusual hat that characterises the person who wears it. Describe the hat and its owner, showing how they link. Describe the person, thinking about their:

- age
- job
- appearance.

✏️ Activity 1 — Understanding the meaning

1) Complete the sentences below by adding the correct form of the word 'characterise'.

   a) If you _____ all teenagers as party animals, you clearly don't know this age group.

   b) The story had excellent _____; the main group of girls were so believable.

   c) It was another _____ warm evening, so they sat outside talking until midnight.

   d) With a _____ shrug, the lonely boy walked away.

2) Write a sentence of your own using the word 'characterise'.

   _____

   _____

Characterise 3

✏ Activity 2   Exploring the meaning

Read the extract below about a sweet shop owner from *Boy* by Roald Dahl.

> She was a small skinny old hag with a moustache on her upper lip and a mouth as sour as a green gooseberry. She never smiled. She never welcomed us when we went in … But by far the most loathsome thing about Mrs Pratchett was the filth that clung around her. Her apron was grey and greasy. Her blouse had bits of breakfast all over it, toast-crumbs and tea stains and splotches of dried egg-yolk.

Fill in the table below to explain the characterisation of this shopkeeper. The first has been completed for you.

Characterisation	Evidence	What these words suggest
bitter	'mouth as sour as a green gooseberry'	Her bitter character will make you wince and shy away, as if an unripe fruit was in your mouth.
unkind		
untidy and dirty		

✏ Activity 3   'Characterise' in context: writing skills

Choose a character and a description from the ideas below.

Character	Description
witch	lazy
musician	kind
chef	forgetful
police officer	bored
superhero	excited

On separate paper, write a description of your character in under 100 words. Think carefully about how you can bring your character to life, just like the example of the sweet shop owner in Activity 2.

63

Chapter 4: Analysis and explanation

4 Portray

The **verb** 'portray' has two meanings:

1) to describe or show a person or thing in a particular way
2) to make a picture of a person or scene.

> She was very upset that the newspapers *portrayed* her as dishonest. (verb)

> The artist *portrayed* her riding her horse. (verb)

Another word in the same **word family** is the **noun** 'portrayal'.

> The actor's *portrayal* of Macbeth was outstanding. (noun)

Word knowledge

'Portray' comes from the Old French *portraire*, meaning 'to draw forth, paint or trace'. This is where the word 'portrait' comes from, meaning 'a picture of the head and face'.

How does the action of drawing or painting something add to your understanding of the word 'portray'?

💬 Have your say

What does an actor have to think about when portraying a character? Think of four things they might do to help them become someone else.

✏️ Activity 1 — Understanding the meaning

1) Read the sentences below and tick those where forms of the word 'portray' are used correctly.

They vowed to keep the girl safe and not portray her to the gang.	
Everyone said the magazine's portrayal of the event did not reflect the day at all.	
The teacher portrayed her time, while marking books on the way home.	
The silent portrayal of fear gripped the whole audience.	

2) Rewrite an incorrect sentence, replacing the form of the word 'portray' with a more suitable alternative.

Portray 4

✏ Activity 2 — Exploring the meaning

Read these exam-style questions and note down what the task is asking for.
The first one has been done for you.

Exam-style question	My own words
In this scene, how does Shakespeare portray the character of Lady Macbeth?	What is Lady Macbeth like and what words does Shakespeare use to create this picture of her?
Explain how the newsreader portrayed the fire.	
How does the sports commentator portray the tension in this match?	

✏ Activity 3 — 'Portray' in context: reading skills

Read the extract below from *Rowan the Strange* by Julie Hearn. In this extract, Rowan is a patient in a hospital. He is watching a rehearsal for a play. Dr von Metzer is playing the villain (a bad character), Captain Hook, but Rowan senses people's dislike of the man.

> And Rowan was right. Nobody booed, and nobody hissed, but discomfort spread, **palpably**, across the hall as von Metzer **recited** his lines. Discomfort tinged with dislike. Had Rowan been able to pick out the faces of hospital staff, out there in the dark, he would have seen a sourness in their expressions that had nothing to do with the character von Metzer was struggling to portray, and everything to do with the man himself.
>
> **palpably** – obviously
> **recited** – repeated words aloud

1) Who is Dr von Metzer trying to portray in this extract?

---

2) What sort of qualities are usually portrayed by a villain in a play? On separate paper, choose some of the qualities from the Tip box and explain how you might use your voice, **expression**, **gestures** and actions to portray them.

Tip

Qualities that characters might portray include: meanness, aggression, kindness, generosity, evil, bravery, cowardice, good humour, greed.

65

Chapter 4: Analysis and explanation

5 Evaluate

The **verb** 'evaluate' means to consider and decide the value or quality of something.

> It's too early to *evaluate* how successful the treatment has been. (verb)

Other words in the same **word family** are:

- evaluation (**noun**)
- re-evaluate (**verb**)
- re-evaluation (**noun**).

> The test scores completely changed Lou's *evaluation* of her abilities. (noun)

> After the storm, we had to *re-evaluate* our travel plans. (verb)

> The locals campaigned for a *re-evaluation* of the speed limit through their town. (noun)

Word knowledge

'Evaluate' comes from the Latin word *valere*, meaning 'to be of value'. The word 're-evaluate' has the **prefix** *re-*, which means 'again'.

How does this help your understanding of the words 'evaluate' and 're-evaluate'?

Have your say

"Evaluation by others is not a guide for me."
— Bruce Lee (martial artist)

1) What do you think this quotation means?
2) Do you agree with the quotation above? Why/Why not?

Try to justify your ideas with examples to support your points.

Activity 1 — Understanding the meaning

Using the information above, complete the following grid with more information about the word 'evaluate'. Some ideas have been added to help you.

Definition	Characteristics
What does the word evaluate mean?	What might someone do if they were evaluating? • Weigh up different ideas

Evaluate

Examples	Non-examples
When might someone evaluate?	What is an example of someone not evaluating? • Not bothering to consider evidence or information

Evaluate 5

✏️ Activity 2 — Exploring the meaning

The word 'evaluate' is often used in exam questions. It means you need to form an opinion or judgement using the evidence available.

Read the exam-style questions below and note down what you would do for each. The first one has been done for you.

Question	What I would do
In this extract, the writer wants the reader to feel sympathy for the main character. Evaluate how successfully this is achieved.	Find the words that suggest sympathy and explore how well they make me feel sad for the character. Look for other clues – like structure and punctuation – and decide if/how they add to my feeling of sympathy.
Evaluate the benefits of these two environments for the local community hall.	
Evaluate how appealing this product is to teenagers.	
The soundtrack to the film tries to make the audience feel scared. Evaluate how successfully this is achieved.	

✏️ Activity 3 — 'Evaluate' in context: reading skills

Read the extract from a student's answer to the following exam-style question:

> **In this extract, the writer wants the reader to feel sympathy for the main character. Evaluate how successfully this is achieved.**

> The words that the writer uses to describe the main character draw attention to his loneliness and sadness. For example, he watches the happy family 'with longing and blinks back tears'. I think the writer is very successful in making the reader feel sympathy for the main character.

Annotate the student's answer to show how they have evaluated the writer's success.

a) Underline the main point and label it 'A'.
b) Circle the quotation that backs up the main point and label it 'B'.
c) Mark the sentence where the student gives their opinion with 'X'.

67

Chapter 4: Analysis and explanation

6 Context

The **noun** 'context' has two meanings:
1) the background situation that helps to explain something
2) the words that come before and after a particular word or phrase and help to make its meaning clear.

> If you take these comments out of *context*, you won't understand what was said. (noun)

> Skilled readers use *context* to understand the meaning of unfamiliar words. (noun)

Other words in the same **word family** are:
- contextual (**adjective**)
- contextualise (**verb**).

> *Contextual* knowledge of WW1 is important to our overall understanding of the poem. (adjective)

> The notes about Victorian London in the introduction help to *contextualise* the novel. (verb)

Contextual knowledge of WW1 is important to our overall understanding of the poem.

Word knowledge

'Context' comes from the Latin word *contexere*, meaning 'join together' or 'weave together'.

How might the meaning of 'join' and 'weave' add to your understanding of the word 'context'?

Have your say

Knowing the context of something can change how we see things. For example, a man breaking into a house could appear to be committing a crime. However, if the context is that the house is on fire and the man is a firefighter, it changes how we see the situation.

Look at the situations below and think about possible contexts. Try to come up with a positive and a negative context for each situation.

- Two dogs barking in a car
- A nurse crying on a pavement

✏ Activity 1 | Understanding the meaning

1) Complete the sentences below by adding the correct form of the word 'context'.

   a) His understanding of the event changed when he heard the _____.

   b) Despite the _____ information, the judge did not change her mind.

   c) I really struggled to _____ my thoughts.

   d) The _____ of the word made the meaning clear.

2) Write a sentence of your own using the word 'context'.

68

Context 6

✏️ Activity 2 — Exploring the meaning

1) The meaning of a word can change depending on its context. Explain the different meanings of the words underlined in the statements below. The first one has been done for you.

   a) The criminals were given long <u>sentences</u> as punishment for their terrible crimes.

   The students found it impossible to follow the long, rambling <u>sentences</u> of the old man.

   > In the first statement, the word 'sentences' refers to prison sentences. In the second statement, the word 'sentences' refers to groups of words.

   b) We'll <u>weave</u> baskets to sell at the craft fair.

   They decided to <u>weave</u> their way through the crowd to reach the stage.

   ----

   c) The <u>mouse</u> scampered away into its nest.

   I struggled to control the <u>mouse</u> with my injured hand and could not access the screen.

   ----

2) Write two sentences of your own, using the same word in different contexts, to show two different meanings. You could choose one of these words:

   mean   **rose**   **address**   **band**   **bark**

   ----

3) When you come across an unfamiliar word, you can often work out its meaning by its context. Read the sentence below. Use the context to work out what the underlined word might mean. Write your answer on separate paper.

   > In the old photograph there was a <u>costermonger</u> on the street, selling a pile of vegetables from a wooden barrow.

   I think the word 'costermonger' might mean --

✏️ Activity 3 — 'Context' in context: writing skills

Choose a dramatic scene or event from one of your favourite books or films. On separate paper, briefly describe what happens in the scene, but also explain the context in which it takes place for someone who is unfamiliar with the story. When describing the context think about:

- where the scene or event takes place
- who the main characters are
- what has happened before
- how important the event or scene is in the overall story.

69

Chapter 4: Analysis and explanation

7 Conventional

The **adjective** 'conventional' means doing things in the normal or accepted way.

> Despite their *conventional* neighbours, they decided to paint the house purple. (adjective)

Other words in the same **word family** are:

- convention (**noun**)
- conventionality (**noun**)
- conventionally (**adverb**).

> In some cultures, a New Year *convention* is to eat twelve grapes. (noun)

> *Conventionality* was something the painter wanted to avoid. (noun)

> He was *conventionally* dressed for the meeting, in shirt and tie. (adverb)

Word knowledge

The word 'conventional' comes from the Latin word *convenire*, which means 'to assemble (come together) or agree'.

How does this information help your understanding of the word 'conventional'?

Activity 1 — Understanding the meaning

Using the information above, complete the following grid with more information about the word 'conventional'. Some ideas have been added to help you.

Definition	Characteristics
What does the word conventional mean?	What does conventional behaviour look like? • Behaving normally
Examples	**Non-examples**
Where might someone see conventional behaviour?	What isn't conventional behaviour? • Doing something out of the ordinary

Conventional

Have your say

1) What does it look like to lead 'a conventional life'?
2) What might be the benefits of a conventional life?

Try to justify your ideas with examples to support your points.

Conventional 7

Activity 2　Exploring the meaning

Look at the word web of synonyms for the adjective 'conventional'. Use the word list on pages 76–78 to look up any unfamiliar words.

Word web: **conventional** — traditional, accepted, orthodox, prosaic, unoriginal, expected

1) Decide whether the synonyms have positive or negative **connotations**. List them in the table below, along with your reasoning. Note that some words may fit in both columns.

Positive connotations	Negative connotations
	unoriginal – suggests boring

2) Choose two of these words, one with positive connotations and one with negative connotations. Write sentences for each of these words, showing their different meanings.

Activity 3　'Conventional' in context: reading skills

Read the extract below from *Looking at the Stars* by Jo Cotterill. Jenna and Amina are escaping from soldiers, but they have become separated from their little sister. The girls usually follow the convention of wearing different coloured headscarves to show who is the oldest. Only the oldest should speak in public.

> I was still wearing Jenna's headscarf. It seemed more sensible, as we both knew I was more confident about speaking to people. But as the day went on, even conventional Jenna abandoned tradition and begged people to tell us if they had seen a little girl with dark eyes and hair.

1) What is meant by 'abandoned tradition'?

----

2) In your own words, describe what you think 'conventional Jenna' might be like.

----

3) Think of the most conventional character you have seen in a film, book or on TV. On separate paper, describe how/why they are conventional.

Chapter 4: Analysis and explanation

8 Imply

The **verb** 'imply' has two meanings:

1) to suggest something without saying it directly
2) to suggest something as an understandable result.

> Her knowledge of video games *implied* that she had been playing for years. (verb)

> Less traffic in the city *implies* a decrease in air pollution. (verb)

Another word in the same **word family** is the **noun** 'implication'.

> The *implication* of the politician's speech is that he's fed up. (noun)

Less traffic in the city **implies** *a decrease in air pollution.*

Word knowledge

'Imply' comes from the Latin word *implicitus*, which means 'folded in'.

How might this Latin meaning add to your understanding of what it means to 'imply'?

💬 Have your say

1) Look at the following actions and consider what they might imply:
   - a frown
   - a wink
   - clapping
   - stamping your feet.
2) What are the dangers in forming an opinion based on implied meaning?

✏️ Activity 1 — Understanding the meaning

1) Complete the sentences below by adding the correct form of the word 'imply'.

   a) We should all be concerned by the _____ that this will be around for years.

   b) The survey _____ that more people are shopping locally instead of online.

   c) His quivering smile _____ that he was nervous about his speech.

   d) The building of a new shopping centre will have _____ for the small local shops.

2) Write a sentence of your own using the word 'imply'.

   _____

   _____

Imply 8

✏ Activity 2 Exploring the meaning

1) What is the meaning implied in each speech bubble?

a) (You're not going out in that are you?)

----

b) (I think you need to look at that answer again.)

----

c) (I suggest we arrange a couple of extra rehearsals.)

----

d) (I don't think she's very happy.)

----

e) (When did you last tidy your room?)

----

2) Read the sentences below. What's implied by each description?

a) He winced and turned away. When he did speak again, his voice was low and unsteady.

----

b) When the teacher asked for a volunteer, most of the students looked at the floor or out of the window.

----

c) When I heard the news, I felt hot and my pulse began to race.

✏ Activity 3 'Imply' in context: writing skills

On separate paper, complete the dialogue below. Three friends, Sam, Rishi and Vineeta, have met in the park. Rishi has a bag of chips. Think carefully about what you can imply about the characters through their speech and actions.

Sam: They look like great chips!

Vineeta: They smell delicious too.

Rishi: (shrugs) They're all right, I suppose.

73

Chapter 4: Analysis and explanation

9 Ambiguous

The **adjective** 'ambiguous' means having more than one possible meaning.

Her message was *ambiguous*; he didn't really know what she meant. (adjective)

Other words in the same **word family** are:
- ambiguity (**noun**)
- ambiguously (**adverb**).

With so much *ambiguity* about the release date, we don't know when to expect the new game. (noun)

She spoke *ambiguously* to avoid revealing the truth. (adverb)

Word knowledge

The word 'ambiguous' comes from the Latin *ambi-* meaning 'both ways'.

How does this information help your understanding of the word 'ambiguous'?

Have your say

Newspapers often create ambiguous headlines to entertain their readers. Look at some of these examples and consider how they are ambiguous. Think about the overall meaning of the headline and how the word order and lack of punctuation can add ambiguity. Have a look at the first example to help you.

COW INJURES FARMER WITH AXE

Due to the phrasing, we don't know who has the axe. It could be the farmer or it could be the cow using the axe as a weapon – unlikely as that sounds!

KIDS MAKE NUTRITIOUS SNACKS

POLICE HELP DOG BITE VICTIM

Activity 1 — Understanding the meaning

1) Read the sentences below and tick those where forms of the word 'ambiguous' are used correctly.

The politician's speech was ambiguous and caused a lot of confusion.	
There was so much ambiguity in the exam questions that the teacher felt it was an unfair test of the students' knowledge and skills.	
Several songs reminded her of the ambiguous holiday in Spain.	
Although she helped on the project, her ambiguous plans left us feeling confused.	
The seasons changed swiftly, scattering ambiguous leaves over the lawn.	

2) Rewrite an incorrect sentence, replacing the form of the word 'ambiguous' with a more suitable alternative.

Ambiguous

Activity 2 Exploring the meaning

1) Look at these phrases and complete the table to note why each of them is ambiguous.

Ambiguous phrase	Why it is ambiguous
I'm watching that fox cub with my binoculars.	
She had never seen a painting quite like this before.	
The chicken is ready to eat.	
Call me a taxi please.	

2) Write one of your own ambiguous phrases or headlines. Think about where the ambiguity comes from; is it a word with more than one meaning, the word order or missing punctuation?

Activity 3 'Ambiguous' in context: reading skills

Poets often use ambiguity in a clever way to make the reader think carefully about the different meanings of words and phrases. Read the poem 'Clockwise' by John Agard below.

I'm your bedside mate.
And I'll let you all
into a secret.
If my **quartz crystal**
didn't **oscillate**
to tune my pulse rate
to ticking tempo,
you'll surely be late.

But I say nothing.
Just sit in my place
as squat as a toad
and keep a straight face,
pointing to time's road.
Tomorrow at dawn,
I'm set to alarm.
May your dreams be deep
when I steal your sleep.

quartz crystal – thin cut piece of mineral designed to vibrate in a clock
oscillate – to keep moving to and fro

On separate paper, explain how the poet uses ambiguity to entertain the reader. Explain the different meanings and ideas triggered by these words and phrases:

- 'clockwise'
- 'keep a straight face'
- 'I'm set to alarm'.

75

Word list

abandon *(verb)*
1 to stop doing something when it becomes impossible
2 to leave someone or something without intending to return

accepted *(adjective)* generally believed to be correct

afraid *(adjective)* frightened or alarmed

antagonist *(noun)* your opponent in a fight or contest

antagonistic *(adjective)* unfriendly or hostile

attitude *(noun)* a way of thinking or feeling about something

austere *(adjective)*
1 very simple and plain; without luxuries
2 an austere person is very strict and serious

barren *(adjective)* land which is not able to produce crops or has no vegetation

belief *(noun)*
1 the feeling that something exists or is true
2 something that a person believes

bias *(noun)* a strong feeling in favour of one person or side and against another; a prejudice

bigotry *(noun)* holding strong and unreasonable opinions and not willing to listen to other people's opinions

blameless *(adjective)* innocent of doing something wrong

cheating *(noun)* an act of trickery

cheerless *(adjective)* gloomy or dreary

combatant *(noun)* someone who takes part in a fight

combative *(noun)* ready to fight or argue

concerned *(adjective)*
1 worried or anxious
2 involved in or affected by something

conscientious *(adjective)* careful and honest about doing your work properly

contrary *(adjective)*
1 completely different or opposed to something
2 awkward and obstinate

cover *(verb)* to place one thing over or round another; to conceal something

creepy *(adjective)* slightly frightening and sinister

cultured *(adjective)* educated to appreciate literature, art, music, etc.

danger *(noun)*
1 the possibility of suffering harm or death or that something bad might happen
2 a bad effect that happens as a result of doing something

deceive *(verb)* to make a person believe something that is not true

dejected *(adjective)* sad or disappointed

depressed *(adjective)* feeling very sad and without hope

dignified *(adjective)* having or showing a serious manner

diligent *(adjective)* careful and hard-working

disconsolate *(adjective)* unhappy and disappointed

discrimination *(noun)* the unfair treatment of different groups of people especially on the grounds of race, age, sex, or disability

dishonesty *(noun)* without honesty or truthfulness

displeased *(adjective)* feeling annoyance

dissatisfied *(adjective)* not satisfied or pleased

double-cross *(verb)* to deceive or cheat someone who thinks you are working with them

doubtless *(adverb)* certainly; without any doubt

down *(adjective)*
1 unhappy or depressed
2 not connected or working properly

downcast *(adjective)*
1 looking downwards
2 sad or dejected

dreary *(adjective)* dull and bleak

educated *(adjective)* showing a high standard of knowledge and culture, as a result of a good education

emotional *(adjective)*
1 causing strong feelings
2 expressing your feelings openly
3 to do with people's feelings

empty *(adjective)*
1 with nothing in it
2 with nobody in it
3 with no meaning or no effect

endless *(adjective)* never stopping; having no end

enduring *(adjective)* lasting over a period of time

enemy *(noun)* a person who is actively opposed or hostile to someone or something

ethical *(adjective)*
1 to do with ethics
2 morally right; honourable

euphoric *(adjective)* feeling intense excitement and happiness

evil *(noun)*
1 wickedness
2 something bad or harmful

exemplary *(adjective)* very good; being a good example to others

exhilarated *(adjective)* feeling very happy and excited

expected *(adjective)* thought of as likely

Word list

exposed *(adjective)*
1 not covered or hidden
2 not sheltered or protected from the weather
3 in a vulnerable position or situation

fearful *(adjective)*
1 afraid or worried
2 causing fear or horror
3 *(informal)* very great or bad

feeling *(noun)*
1 the ability to feel things; the sense of touch
2 what a person feels in the mind; emotion
3 what you think about something

ferocity *(noun)* violence or fierceness

focused *(adjective)* directing attention, interest, or activity towards a particular aim

foe *(noun)* an enemy

forecast *(verb)* to say in advance what is likely to happen

forego *(verb)* to decide to give something up; to go without something

foreground *(noun)* the part of a scene, picture or view that is nearest to you

foresee *(verb)* to realise that something is likely to happen

foreshadow *(verb)* to be a sign of something that is to come

forewarn *(verb)* to warn someone beforehand

foreword *(noun)* a short introduction at the beginning of a book

forfeit *(verb)* to pay or give up something as a penalty

formal *(adjective)*
1 strictly following the accepted rules or customs; not casual
2 rather serious and stiff in your manner
3 official or ceremonial

fraud *(noun)*
1 the crime of getting money by tricking people
2 a dishonest trick
3 a person who is not what they pretend to be

fruitless *(adjective)* producing no results

glum *(adjective)* miserable or depressed

guile *(noun)* craftiness and deceit

hard-working *(adjective)* working with energy and commitment; diligent

hazard *(noun)* a danger or risk

heartless *(adjective)* cruel or without pity

honourable *(adjective)* able to be trusted and always trying to do the right thing; deserving honour and respect

humane *(adjective)* showing kindness and a wish to cause as little suffering or pain as possible

imperfect *(adjective)*
1 with faults or problems; not perfect
2 the imperfect tense of a verb shows a continuous action in the past, e.g. She was singing.

inability *(noun)* being unable to do something

inaction *(noun)* lack of action where some is expected or appropriate

inadequate *(adjective)*
1 not enough; not good enough
2 not able to cope or deal with something intense

incessant *(adjective)* continuing for a long time without a pause

inconsiderate *(adjective)* thoughtlessly causing hurt or inconvenience to others

jeopardy *(noun)* danger of harm or failure

jittery *(adjective)* extremely nervous and anxious

junior *(adjective)*
1 younger
2 for young children
3 lower in rank or importance

low-grade *(adjective)* of low quality or standard

madness *(noun)*
1 the state of having a serious mental illness
2 extremely foolish behaviour
3 a state of wild activity

malevolent *(adjective)* showing a desire to harm other people

malformed *(adjective)* faultily formed

malfunction *(noun)* faulty functioning

malicious *(adjective)* intending to do harm

malnutrition *(noun)* bad health because you do not have enough food or the right kind of food

malodorous *(adjective)* smelling very unpleasant

malpractice *(noun)* careless, wrong or illegal behaviour while in a professional job

maltreat *(verb)* to ill-treat a person or animal

mask *(verb)*
1 to cover your face with a mask
2 to disguise or conceal something

mediocre *(adjective)* not very good; of only medium quality

menacing *(adjective)* threatening to cause harm or danger

mislead *(verb)* to give someone the wrong idea or impression

mournful *(adjective)* sad and sorrowful

narrow-mindedness *(noun)* the state of being unaccepting of other people's beliefs and ways

nervous *(adjective)*
1 anxious about something or afraid of something
2 easily worried or frightened
3 to do with the nerves

nostalgic *(adjective)* feeling pleasure, mixed with sadness, when you remember happy times in the past

offer up *(verb)* to give something to a god

ominous *(adjective)* suggesting that trouble is coming

opinion *(noun)* what you think of something; a belief or judgement

Word list

opponent *(noun)* a person or group opposing another in a contest or war

orthodox *(adjective)*
1 holding beliefs that are correct or generally accepted
2 conventional or normal

pensive *(adjective)* deep in thought

pitfall *(noun)* a hidden danger or difficulty

polite *(adjective)* having good manners; showing respect to other people

preconception *(noun)* an idea without knowing all the facts

pretence *(noun)* an attempt to pretend that something is true

principled *(adjective)* having strong beliefs about what is right and wrong; based on strong beliefs

productive *(adjective)*
1 producing a lot of things
2 producing good results; useful

prosaic *(adjective)* plain or dull and ordinary

rage *(noun)* great or violent anger

reflective *(adjective)*
1 providing a reflection
2 thoughtful

relentless *(adjective)* not stopping or letting up

remorseless *(adjective)* without regret or guilt

renounce *(verb)* to give up or reject something

risk *(noun)* a chance that something bad will happen

rival *(noun)* a person or thing that competes with another or tries to do the same thing

savagery *(noun)* the quality of being fierce or cruel

secrete *(verb)*
1 to hide something
2 to produce a substance in the body

sentimental *(adjective)*
1 connected with your emotions, rather than reason
2 producing emotions like love, or being sad, which may be too strong or not appropriate; feeling these emotions too much

sickly *(adjective)*
1 often ill; unhealthy
2 making people feel sick
3 weak or sentimental

sombre *(adjective)*
1 dark in colour
2 gloomy or serious

sophisticated *(adjective)*
1 a sophisticated person has refined or cultured tastes and is experienced about life
2 complicated and advanced

stash *(verb)* to store something safely in a secret place

steadfast *(adjective)* firm and not changing

stern *(adjective)* strict and severe; not smiling

stow *(verb)* to pack or store something away

subordinate *(adjective)*
1 less important
2 lower in rank

surrender *(verb)*
1 to stop fighting and give yourself up to an enemy
2 to hand something over to another person, especially when forced to do so

tactless *(adjective)* having or showing a lack of tact; not caring if you offend someone

tenacious *(adjective)*
1 holding or clinging firmly to something
2 obstinate and persistent

thought *(noun)*
1 something that you think; an idea or opinion
2 the process of thinking

threatening *(adjective)* having a frightening quality or manner

tireless *(adjective)* having a lot of energy; not tiring easily

tolerant *(adjective)* willing to accept or put up with other people's behaviour and opinions even if you do not agree with them

traditional *(adjective)*
1 passed down from one generation to another
2 following older methods and ideas rather than modern ones

trick *(verb)* to deceive or cheat someone by a trick

trickery *(noun)* the use of tricks; deception

turbulence *(noun)* violent and uneven movement of air or water

uncertainty *(noun)*
1 the state of being uncertain
2 something that you cannot be sure about; a situation that makes you not be or feel certain

uneasy *(adjective)*
1 worried or anxious
2 uncomfortable

unoriginal *(adjective)* not new; uninteresting

unwelcoming *(adjective)*
1 not friendly towards somebody who is visiting or arriving
2 not attractive; looking uncomfortable to be in

veil *(verb)*
1 to cover something with a veil
2 to partially conceal something

view *(noun)*
1 what you can see from one place, e.g. beautiful scenery
2 sight or range of vision
3 an opinion

worthy *(adjective)* deserving respect or support

wrath *(noun)* extreme anger

Key terms glossary

adjective a word that describes a person, place or object (nouns and pronouns)

adverb a word that gives more detail about a verb, an adjective or another adverb

antonym a word meaning the opposite of another word, e.g. 'good' is an antonym for 'bad'

connotation an idea or meaning suggested by a word or phrase

context the parts of a text that come immediately before and after a word and clarify its meaning, or the background against which something happens

direct address where a writer or speaker is talking directly to an individual or group

emotive language words that create a particular emotional reaction from the reader

expression the look on a person's face that shows his or her feelings

first person a type of narrative where the main character tells their story using 'I'

gesture a movement that expresses what a person feels

metaphor describing something as something else, not meant to be taken literally, e.g. 'You are a star.'

mood the atmosphere or tone of something

noun a word used to name a person, place, idea or thing

past tense a tense used to describe things that have already happened

personification representing an idea in human form or a thing as having human characteristics e.g. 'The daffodils danced in the wind.'

plot the story in a play, novel or film

plural noun a noun that is more than one. Most plural nouns are made by adding '-s' or '-es' to the singular noun, e.g. 'foxes' or 'hats'

posture the position in which you hold your body when you stand, sit or walk

prefix a group of letters placed in front of a root word to add to or change its meaning, e.g. 'un-' or 'dis-'

pronoun a word that can be used instead of a noun

rhetorical question a question asked for dramatic effect and not intended to get an answer

root word a word in its most basic form, e.g. 'look'

rule of three (also called 'tricolon') linking three points or features for impact

setting the time and place where the action of a story happens

suffix a group of letters that can be added to the end of the root form of a word, e.g. '-ed' or '-ing'

synonym a word that means the same or almost the same as another word, e.g. 'glad' is a synonym for 'happy'

tone the way a writer expresses his or her attitude to the subject

verb a word that identifies actions, thoughts, feelings or a state of being

word family a group of words that have the same root word which can be changed by adding different prefixes and suffixes

OXFORD
UNIVERSITY PRESS

Great Clarendon Street, Oxford, OX2 6DP, United Kingdom

Oxford University Press is a department of the University of Oxford.

It furthers the University's objective of excellence in research, scholarship, and education by publishing worldwide. Oxford is a registered trade mark of Oxford University Press in the UK and in certain other countries

Copyright © Oxford University Press 2021

The moral rights of the author have been asserted

First published in 2021

All rights reserved. No part of this publication may be reproduced, stored in a retrieval system, or transmitted, in any form or by any means, without the prior permission in writing of Oxford University Press, or as expressly permitted by law, by licence or under terms agreed with the appropriate reprographics rights organization. Enquiries concerning reproduction outside the scope of the above should be sent to the Rights Department, Oxford University Press, at the address above.

You must not circulate this work in any other form and you must impose this same condition on any acquirer

British Library Cataloguing in Publication Data
Data available

ISBN 978-138-201423-6

10 9 8 7 6 5 4 3 2

Paper used in the production of this book is a natural, recyclable product made from wood grown in sustainable forests.

The manufacturing process conforms to the environmental regulations of the country of origin.

Printed in Great Britain by Bell and Bain Ltd., Glasgow

Acknowledgements
We are grateful for permission to include the following copyright material:

John Agard: 'Clockwise' from *Hello H2O* (Hodder Children's Books, 2013), copyright © John Agard 2003, reprinted by permission of Hodder Children's Books, an imprint of Hachette Children's Books, Carmelite House, 50 Victoria Embankment, London EC4 Y 0DZ.

Terence Blacker: extract from 'Lady in Blue Unidentified', copyright © Terence Blacker 1994, first published in *Ghostly Haunts* edited by Michael Morpurgo (HarperCollins, 1994), reprinted by permission of Terence Blacker c/o Caroline Sheldon Literary Agency Ltd.

Malorie Blackman: extract from *Noble Conflict* (Corgi, 2014), copyright © Malorie Blackman 2013, reprinted by permission of The Random House Group Ltd, Penguin Random House UK.

Steve Connor: extract from 'Forty years since the first picture of earth from space', *The Independent*, 10 January 2009, copyright © Steve Connor/ The Independent 2009, reprinted by permission of ESI Media for Independent Digital News and Media Ltd.

Jo Cotterill: extract from *Looking at the Stars* (Corgi, 2015), copyright © Jo Cotterill 2014, reprinted by permission of The Random House Group Ltd, Penguin Random House UK.

Roald Dahl: extract from 'The Bicycle and the Sweetshop' from *Boy – Tales of Childhood* (Puffin, 2013), copyright © The Roald Dahl Story Company Ltd 1984, reprinted by permission of David Higham Associates.

Leon Garfield: extract from *Smith* (Puffin, 2014), copyright © Leon Garfield 1967, reprinted by permission of the Estate of Leon Garfield c/o Johnson & Alcock Ltd.

Julie Hearn: extract from *Rowan the Strange* (OUP, 2010), copyright © Julie Hearn 2010, reprinted by permission of Oxford University Press through PLSclear.

Geraldine McCaughrean: extract from *Where the World Ends* (Usborne, 2017), copyright © Geraldine McCaughrean 2017, reprinted by permission of David Higham Associates.

Douglas McPherson: extract from 'Think twice before voting for against animal circuses', *The Telegraph*, 16 April 2010, copyright © Douglas McPherson/Telegraph Media Group Ltd 2010, reprinted by permission of TMG Ltd.

Darren Simpson: extract from *Scavengers* (Usborne, 2019), copyright © Darren Simpson 2019, reprinted by permission of Usborne Publishing, 83-85 Saffron Hill, London EC1n 8RT, www.usborne.com.

Robert Swindells: extract from *Room 13* (Yearling, 1990), copyright © Robert Swindells 1989, reprinted by permission of The Random House Group Ltd, Penguin Random House UK.

David Walliams: extract from 'Roald Dahl and Me', *The Independent*, 4 Nov 2009, copyright © David Walliams/The Independent 2009, reprinted by permission of ESI Media for Independent Digital News and Media Ltd.

Emma Watson: extract from 'HeForShe' campaign launch speech given at the United Nations, 20 Sept 2014, reprinted by permission of Emma Watson.

The publisher and author would like to thank the following for permission to use photographs and other copyright material:

Cover: Robyn Mackenzie/Shutterstock; Nata Kuprova/Shutterstock; Alisa_Elly/Shutterstock. **Photos: p1:** Robyn Mackenzie/Shutterstock; **p61(l):** Painterstock/Shutterstock; **p61(r):** Boyan Dimitrov/Shutterstock.

Artwork by Jess McGeachin, Aptara, Oxford University Press, and Oxford University Press ANZ.

Every effort has been made to contact copyright holders of material reproduced in this book. Any omissions will be rectified in subsequent printings if notice is given to the publisher.

Word list definitions are based on the definitions from *Oxford School Dictionary*.